1. What's Next?

There is one thing entrepreneurs can never lose sight of. **What is true today may not be true tomorrow.** If this past year has taught us anything it is this: Change is inevitable. Stuff happens. Yesterday's news is exactly that ... yesterday's news. How you choose to spend your time today will determine the resultant smile on your face in all your tomorrows.

Here is another fact we can agree with. There is no shortage of *advice* coming from the mouths, offices and websites of self-labeled industry gurus. Be careful of who you put your faith in.

But getting back to the title in chapter number one, "What's next?"

Regardless of your current situation, if I were asked for a one word answer it would sound a lot like the word "prospecting." **Prospecting** will always be the key to one's business success. I suppose two more words that support this future business-building challenge would be **"Lead Generation."**

PRE-REQUISITE: Before spending your time trying to identify new and exciting business opportunities, you will be well-advised to cement the relationships you already have with your "valued" clients of today. Remember, your customer is my prospect. Protect your current assets.

FACT: The sooner you internalize the importance of seeking new business opportunities, the sooner you will be sowing the seeds for a profitable future.

Back To Prospecting.
To help you simplify this prospecting thing, you can divide the population of our planet into two categories. Nearly eight billion people reside on our planet, and you can divide them into just two groups.

Group 1: People you can help.
Group 2: People you can't help.

Once you begin looking at your personal marketplace through this new lens, your job will immediately make sense to you.

Your job becomes identifying individuals you can help. How you choose to do this is up to you, but I believe the most efficient way is by trying to find out who has a genuine interest in your particular area of expertise. Manage to get "prospects" to raise their hand indicating interest in you and your expertise. Then, supply them with valuable information designed to "scratch their itch."

I am reminded of the very sage advice, "When the student is ready, th4 teacher appears." This is exactly what you are attempting to do … get interested would-be travelers to raise their hand.

You can use your phone, email, snail mail, or meet with groups of people to ask them if they would like to learn more about your specialty. If this sounds too simplistic then you are

 Welcome back. This is Volume 2 in the series titled **I'm Just Sayin'**. My name is still Mike Marchev, as I found no reason to enter the witness protection program after publishing the first 57 articles in this project. In fact, after rereading all 57 messages in Volume 1, I found myself saying to myself, ***"This stuff isn't too bad."***

To the contrary. The information in Volume 1 was pretty darn good ... on-target and meaningfully entertaining. It prompted me to get busy compiling these 57 additional reminders, suggestions, recommendations and lessons designed to help you, the reader, become more successful.

It has been said that I write like I talk. Being the optimistic lad that I am, I take this to be a positive observation. This reputation, in and of itself, allows me the freedom to screw up the King's English now and then while periodically salting in a few words that may be missing, or purposely overlooked in Mr. Webster's Dictionary.

I think it was Louis Pasteur, or perhaps Einstein himself, who once said between experiments, "You can take the boy out of New Jersey, but come hell or high water, he will always be a product of Exit 135." (Don't quote me on that. It might have been the x-Dodger Manager, Leo Durocher.)

Read them. Don't read them. Skim them. Internalize them. The choice is yours. But always remember that your future is just that... your future. If you ask me, I strongly recommend you read all 57 ... twice. Find time to think about each lesson found within. Reflect accordingly. Then get your two rosy cheeks out of the chair and back to making your life one you can be proud of.

Table of Contents

1. What's Next? 5
2. The Ideal Sales Strategy 9
3. Stuff Happens 11
4. Be Happening! 13
5. Selling Is No Longer a Numbers Game 15
6. You Don't Have to Like "Everybody" 19
7. Believe It or Not, Stress Is an Option 22
8. Marketing Works ... *But Only If You Do* 24
9. Respond To Leads Promptly 26
10. TGIT: Thank Goodness It's Today! 28
11. Sometimes Things Actually Do Work 30
12. Stop. Think. Act. 32
13. It Isn't Over Until It Is Over 34
14. Your Tone Speaks Volumes 36
15. You Market for Tomorrow 39
16. You Didn't Get This Far by Accident! 41
17. The Importance of Leading a Disciplined Life 43
18. Take Responsibility for Your Future. 45
19. Multitasking Is a Game for Losers 47
20. A Gentle "Wake Up Call" Might Be in Order 49
21. Clarity of Intention 51
22. Are You "Laughing & Scratching" Regularly? 53
23. Stop Worrying and Just Hit the Ball 55
24. A Lesson from Your Morning Crossword Puzzle 57

25. Read That Book Again 59
26. Crossword Puzzles and Books 61
27. Don't Stop Thinking About Tomorrow 63
28. Elephants Don't Bite 65
29. Failure Is Not Something to Avoid 67
30. I Love It When a Plan Comes Together 69
31. You Can't Tell a Book by Its Cover 72
32. The Next One Could Be the Big One 74
33. Podcasts "R" Us 76
34. Simple Is Better 78
35. Some Ideas Are Worth Repeating 80
36. There's No Such Thing As "Down-Time" 82
37. The Path to Success Is Usually Less Travelled 84
38. Nobody Owes You a Living 87
39. Don't Bite Off More Than You Can Chew 89
40. Choose Your Words Wisely 91
41. Execution 93
42. Marketing Strategy #7: The Interview 95
43. Lessons From a Fabric Store 98
44. Are You Climbing Up the Wrong Ladder? 100
45. Repetition Is Not a Bad Thing 102
46. Are You Protecting Your Greatest Asset? 104
47. Don't "Throw In The Towel?" Not Yet! 106
48. Three "Brilliant" Reminders 109
49. Some Good Advice for Job Seekers 112
50. Cool Your Jets! 115
51. In Search of That Elusive "One Thing" 117

52. From Annoying Pest to Welcome Guest 119
53. Follow Up Never Goes Out of Style 121
54. What Do Gutters Have to Do with Anything? 124
55. My Thoughts on Integrity Selling 126
56. "Lazy" Is Not a Flattering Characteristic 128
57. Are You Becoming Lazy? Part Two 130
Five of My Favorite Quotes: 132

reading me correctly. It sounds simple because it is simple. It is simple because it is logical.

Personally, I offer a "Special Report" to accomplish this task. It might sound something like this: *"If you would like to learn how you can double your business in the next twelve months (really) I have a document you might want to read. It is titled My 12-Word Marketing Plan."* *(That is step #1.)*

Readers who send me an email requesting my report are clearly indicating they are interested in learning how to expand their client base. They are raising their hand and voluntarily positioning themselves as potential prospects.

(Step #2.) I send them the requested information giving them a written document to judge me by. They get a feel for my personality along with my knowledge of the subject matter and my communication style. I follow up giving them time to internalize my information and eventually something happens. By "something" I mean either a budding relationship begins, or I realize they are not interested in me or the horse I rode in on. I classify them accordingly and file their contact information.

If there is a secret to this prospecting thing it is to do it daily, regularly… and consistently. Keep your eyes and ears open for opportunities where you can ask *"Are you interested in learning more about…"*

You will sabotage your efforts if you (1) postpone your prospecting campaign, or (2) initiate a hit or miss program with days, weeks, or months between inactivity.

I'm telling you your next "profitable" client is out there. You just have to go find them. You must keep looking. You can't stop looking until you find them. They are out there. Honest!

> "When the student is ready, the teacher appears."

2. The Ideal Sales Strategy

The state was New Mexico. The time was a few years back. The place was an automobile dealership. The gig was sales training.

I was invited to share a few of my ideas and proven selling tactics to a room full of professional salespeople. Their sales goal was to move 300 cars every month. (Every month.) It was clear to me that I was not speaking to room full of amateurs.

What caught my curiosity was that every person in the room carried a silver coin in their pocket reminding them that they were the best in the business. The one-word engraved on each coin was **Loyalty**.

This word was driven home in every sales meeting as their single objective was to maintain their current customer list for a long time. Their goal might have been 300 cars, but their results were determined by how well their current clients kept coming back.

TREAT YOUR CLIENTS AS IF THEY HOLD THE KEYS TO YOUR FUTURE ... because they do.

We often treat our neighbor's children with more respect than we treat our own children. We are often more polite to strangers than we are to our loved ones. We go out of our way for prospects more readily than we reach out to our valued clients. This is strange behavior no matter how you slice it.

The winners in a winning organization are the customers. They need to be treated as if the company sincerely wants them to return.

Customer loyalty is fast becoming a thing of the past. Just like my new friends in New Mexico, do not allow this to happen to you. Hold onto your loyal clients and don't ever let them go.

Focus on the needs of your current client base and make it your business to hold on to every single one. Build your business based on a 100% satisfaction level of those you are currently doing business with.

****You might want to do yourself a favor by selecting a reminder of your own and carry it with you to remind you throughout the day that customers hold the key to your future success.

> Treat your clients as if they hold the keys to your future.
>
> (Because they do.)

3. Stuff Happens

Summer thunderstorms have a way of creating havoc. One minute you have electricity. In a blink of an eye and without warning you find yourself powerless. (Without juice.) BAM! Lights out.

This is another example of how quickly things change… and can change … and do change … and will change. One minute you are sailing nicely downwind and before you can say "coming about" you are sitting "high and dry" on a sandbar. One minute you have all the business you can handle; the next your pipeline is drier than an Arizona summer's day. One minute life is grand…then your upcoming weekend becomes disrupted with an unexpected phone call from a distant relative. I'm certain you have a dozen or more examples of your own.

Stuff happens. The lights went out in Georgia… and you might want to stop long enough to locate that flashlight sooner rather than later. Someday… one day… your lights will go out. My question to you is will you be prepared to handle it?

Ask yourself, what is the absolute worst thing that could happen in the next few days, weeks, months? Then, do everything in your power to make it your business that it doesn't happen.

Here are a few examples to help stimulate your preparation.

Worse Thing	What To Do Now
Pulled back muscle	Stretch more often (daily)
Lost account	Call them now
Spouse leaves you	Roses and dinner
Kid gets on drug	Take in a ballgame
Get fired (1)	Get to work earlier
Get fired (2)	Begin networking campaign
Get fired (3)	Celebrate
A blackout	Buy flashlight batteries now
Roof leaks	Patch and replace ASAP
Pets run away	Fix hole in the fence
You trip and fall in the garage	Clean it up once and for all
You can't find important papers	Organize and clean files

You don't have to be caught in the dark if you just exercise a little emotional intelligence. Just do everything you can today to make sure bad "stuff" does not happen to you tomorrow. This simple exercise will position you as a truly exceptional person.

PS. To avoid losing any business as result of a computer crash, back up your important files today. *And store them off property.*

> "What's the worst thing that could happen to you and your business?
>
> (What can you do about it to prevent it from happening today?)

4. Be Happening!

A few years back I visited my high school to spend a day with the senior class. One of my recommendations was to avoid negative people at all cost. Why? Because *"Misery loves company."* No truer words have ever been spoken.

Do not fall into the web of down-trodden, whining, bummed-out, woe is me, life is unfair individuals. The world has its share of people who prefer the role of victim. Don't just walk away from these misguided people ... *RUN AWAY.*

The flip side to this advice is to migrate toward **happening** people. When you come across a person full of ideas who is not frightened to try new things, make an attempt to hitch your wagon to these stabilizing forces and be open to explore the ensuing possibilities.

The power of positive people, optimistic views, and energizing comments is an uplifting phenomenon. Talking to a positive person on the phone or enjoying a few minutes of their company tends to lift your spirits. Just yesterday I spent time with an 85-year-old woman, (high heels and all,) who had the mind and quick wit of today's 30-year-old. Our time together was both refreshing and invigorating. What a joy to be around people like this.

I have a number of associates I contact on a regular basis and before long I find myself laughing, cajoling and brainstorming myself right out of a less-than-positive mood. It works every time.

So, if you find yourself heading for "*Rutsville*" make a call to a member of your "A-Team" and *snap out of it*. We are all in this thing together, and we will all get out of this thing together. Try something new. Attempt something bold. **BE HAPPENING!**

One more thing before you head out to clean the grill. When somebody calls you, it may be a disguised call for help ... an opportunity to pump some hope back into their world. Answer the phone this week like you have it together. There are people out there who need you. And there is a good chance that they are counting on you to help lift their spirits. Don't let them down. Nobody is better at this than you.

Starting tomorrow you can begin showcasing the brand new "*HAPPENING*" you. *Be "happening."*

> You can't fix seasoned, experienced and highly qualified people who insist on focusing on the negative aspects of their unfair existence. Don't try."

5. Selling Is No Longer a Numbers Game

Selling was once believed to be a numbers game. You have undoubtedly heard this popular, weather-beaten career-changing sales advice before. Make the calls, make the presentations, work your way through enough people, and eventually you will make a sale. I'm fast to admit this is not totally false. Raw volume, however, does not necessarily produce success. And even if it did, it would do nothing to enhance your professional reputation.

Rather than thinking of sales as a game of numbers, I want you to begin thinking of sales as **"a game of darts."** By aiming your effort (the dart) at a clearly defined target (your pre-qualified prospect dart board) your chances for hitting the mark (a sale) are greatly enhanced. Contrast that mindset with a pure numbers game where you buy a lottery ticket on a whim and a prayer, or throw a handful of marbles up in the air hoping one or two land in a paper cup.

If you want to save yourself a lot of time, money and frustration, know who you would like to do business with. That's right. I want you to define your target audience. Your chances for success are much higher if you direct your efforts conscientiously toward a list of defined prospects. This concept is known as "Target Marketing."

Example:
Tell me you want to do business with the Pastor of your church, Reverend Jones; your local wine merchant Mr. Chardonnay; The couple down the street, Mary and Tyler what's-their-name?

To help explain the concept, I will refer to the process as "bracketing." Bracketing is a systematic approach for zeroing in on a designated target. Let's use a golfing example of bracketing in action.

During a Merrill Lynch corporate golf outing I once attended in Tucson, Arizona, Al Geiberger was the guest PGA golf professional. He was positioned on a par 3 hole as each foursome of company representatives played through. Al's job as the guest pro was to hit a fifth ball on behalf of the team to win a "closest-to-the-pin" prize.

Prior to the first group arriving at the designated hole, I saw Al hit a single shot to check the distance, wind and firmness of the green. (He was firing his first shot to get a lay of the land.) His initial attempt fell short and to the left of the flagstick. Mr. Geiberger mentally recorded the results. After making a few mechanical adjustments he hit a second ball and watched its flight. This time the ball landed a little long and to the right of the flagstick. Again, he adjusted his mechanics. His third shot was pin high and left. After making the final adjustment, his fourth shot was right on the money. After mentally recording and locking in the swing mechanics for shot #4, he duplicated the shot time and again coming within a few feet from the hole. This impressed the bejabbers out of each passing foursome.

This is how bracketing works — a trial and error, adjustment setting exercise designed to zero in on a given target. Bracketing in sales works the same way. First, you have to lob some effort in the direction of a specific goal (your specified prospect). Then pay attention to what happens. Make a necessary adjustment and try it again. Keep on tweaking your strategy until you hit on a method that results in the prospect becoming a client.

While I have your attention, here is a sales exercise you can experiment with:

> (1) Make a list of five qualified prospects you would like to do business with.
> (2) Write down three ways you can initiate awareness of your products or services among these prospects.
> (3) Initiate your awareness program and record your results from the first-round attempt.
> (4) Make your necessary adjustments to the program and try again (either on the same five prospects or on a new set of five).
> (5) Record and adjust again. Continue until you are, as the pros say, in the zone.
> (6) Finally, apply your refined method to a new group of targeted prospects.

Caution: Bracketing will not necessarily work with prospects you have not qualified. Shooting from the hip will have you back playing the old lottery numbers game. Trying to bracket unqualified prospects is like Al Geiberger trying to drop his shot near the hole when the winds gust on and off up to 40 miles per hour coming from a different direction at any given time. Similarly, unqualified prospects are coming from all different directions in terms of what they want and need. You'll miss the green and become discouraged in no time.

Allow others to waste their time chasing raw numbers. Identify your target and with bracketing as your guiding strategy, become successful by design. There will be very little luck to your new sales campaign.

6. You Don't Have to Like "Everybody"

Today I'm going to introduce you to a popular sales myth. Bear with me on this one since it may rub you the wrong way at first. I think you will soon be agreeing with me.

Many people preach that a prerequisite for becoming successful in sales is to "like people." The implication here is you should have the innate capacity and desire to cozy up to just about anybody who can fog a mirror . . . or at least anybody with a fat wallet. I am not a fan of this postulate. Let me explain.

I have traversed the United States many times, worked in nineteen countries on five continents, and observed countless people on airplanes, in post office lines, at restaurants, toll booths, and department store customer service counters. I have watched people drive cars, run races, attend classes, and root for their kids at high school athletic programs. For over seventy years I have watched people do just about everything people can conceivably do on this planet. (Well . . . almost everything.)

Here is what I have concluded: The world has its quota of boring, insincere, dishonest and negative people who I consciously choose to have nothing to do with. More accurately stated, I don't like them or endorse what they stand for. I have no intention or desire of entering their world or trying to change them.

On the other hand, during these same travels, I have met many fine, upstanding, fun and creative human beings trying to creatively figure out how things work while maintaining a refreshing sense of humor and appreciation for life itself. These people are the ones I choose to be around . . . learn from . . . and try to emulate. I like these people. I guess what I am saying is **I like the people I like.**

Let's give this "you've got to like people" notion a slight twist. If you want to minimize your stress, have more fun and earn more money, begin spending more time looking for, and doing business with, people you have a natural attraction for . . . people who are honest, hardworking, fun, intelligent, enthusiastic and easy to be around.

It does make sense however, to take some time to understand people better. After all, many nice people just don't know how to make a good first impression. It would be a shame for you to prematurely cross them off your list simply because they are experiencing a bad hair day.

You may feel a little out of sorts right now while thinking to yourself, "Is this guy saying that it is okay to be prejudiced?" No! That it not what I am saying. Not at all.

Take a deep breath and read the above again. I am saying that it is okay if you don't do business with rude, unhappy, belly-aching whiners. That is what I am saying, and I will say it in a court of law if you insist on hearing it under oath.

Where does it say you must do business with (or worse, seek business from) everyone who wants your service or product? That's a myth.

If you are going to service people to the full extent of your capabilities, you might as well do it for people who appreciate your contributions and hard work. This alone will result in more energy and a positive attitude. And that my friends translates to a happier you and a more successful business.

7. Believe It or Not, Stress Is an Option

Another myth often associated with the selling profession is that stress, like rejection, is inevitable. It is true the two often "travel" together weighing down the carrier. The truth also is that stress is not absolutely necessary.

Without exception everyone acknowledges they experience some level of stress in their lives. They seem to accept stress as a common debilitation given at birth, and they often have been heard bragging about it. (Strange behavior.)

It's true that a lot of sales professionals exhibit stress at times. But stress does not have to rule your life. You were not born with stress, like the color of your eyes. It is something that you allow to happen along life's circuitous path. Stress is self-imposed in many if not most instances and is a by-product of pretending that the world operates differently than it actually does.

When our imperfect world, on whose game board we all must function follows its natural course, we object to its imperfections and thereby fuel our personal stress level. In engineering, stress results from the application of a constant force to an immovable object. In life, the force is your **expectations**. The object is **reality**. You pretend . . . you guess wrong . . . you get stressed. Once you learn to go with the natural flow and rhythms of the world (by all means stopping long enough to change what can be changed), you will become more effective, efficient and pleasant to be around.

Starting today, begin accepting our imperfect world for what it is ... imperfect. Change what you can but stop becoming befuddled with what you have no control over.

8. Marketing Works ... *But Only If You Do*

I don't consider myself an impulse buyer, but I once purchased a vacuum cleaner from a TV infomercial .... *at 3:30 am.*

I am usually asleep at 3:30 am, but on this particular night in a Kansas City hotel I found it difficult to fall asleep. I was wide awake watching television when an infomercial caught my attention. Before I knew it, I was the proud owner of a vacuum cleaner known as **The Stick Shark**. This thing sucks up screws and bolts like nothing you have ever seen. *How did that happen?*

Later that week...
I read about a new book titled **The Tipping Point** in the New York Times, by Malcolm Gladwell. It looked like something I might be interested in, but I didn't give it another thought ... until I found myself browsing at a Barnes & Noble Book Store & Café on a Saturday afternoon, when I spotted that very same title in the business section. I was soon the owner of **The Tipping Point**. *How did that happen?*

In both instances, "it" happened because the product was brought to my attention. In both instances, a product was introduced to me, and I was given a few reasons why I might want to consider buying the item in question. I was not shopping for a vacuum cleaner nor does my office library need another business book. It wasn't my idea to purchase either of these products ... until the product was brought to my attention.

These are two examples of how marketing works. Granted, it doesn't work all the time on every single prospect, but in the long run, it works. But I can promise you that it won't work unless you do. **And here is what you have to do.**

1. You must introduce yourself and your service to targeted people in your marketplace. In the majority of cases, more than once.
2. Give them a few good reasons why they would be better off having you as their service provider.
3. Allow the cards to fall where they may and follow-up when necessary.

Not every sleep-deprived traveling marketing guy provided their credit card number at 3:30 a.m. so they could be the proud owner of a bolt-sucking vacuum named after a fish. But I did. Marketing works folks ... but only if you give it a chance to work.

Here is what I want you to do. Get out and make it your business to connect with more people in your targeted audience. Tell them what you have to offer. Tell them what is in it for them. Some people will pay attention. Some people won't. And a few may even become your next client. (Stranger things have happened. I am proof of that.)

> "You will miss 100% of the shots you don't take."

9. Respond To Leads Promptly

Here is a quote from a book I read titled **DO IT MARKETING** by David Newman. **"When it comes to responding to leads, the mantra is 'Now or Never.' Leads won't wait. They are looking for a solution NOW."**

Regardless of the current condition of your business, leads are your key focal point when it comes to growing your business. Without leads you have no business-development plan. Without leads you become complacent and find yourself tending to your business as usual. Without leads you become lethargic and even boring. Yes, leads are the lifeblood of a growing business. **Generate more leads.**

Why is speed so important? Once a lead enters the picture, an imaginary timer begins a countdown. It becomes imperative that you respond to your lead in an expeditious fashion. Remember the window of opportunity does not remain open for long.

There are too many options available to consumers today. They have little time or patience trying to empathize with your lethargy. I have found through experience the first supplier to respond to a lead has a definite leg-up on the competition. Speed wins.

Be the first to respond.

The reason you are contacted in the first place is because the prospect feels you are in position to help them. You are just one of many qualified options they can call. You need to recognize this as a huge opportunity and take advantage of this fleeting sign of interest and respond accordingly... with great haste, interest and sincerity.

In most cases the lead is seeking immediate gratification. They are reaching out for information and chances are their lack of patience will dictate their actions. The simple fact that you responded to them quickly is a clear sign that they are important to you. Among dozens of other self-serving traits, people (both you and me) like to feel important.

Leads won't wait for you. They usually cool in very short order. You can't allow this to happen. Remember David's reminder cited above: **"Now or never."**

> "I have found through experience the first supplier to respond to a lead has a definite leg-up on the competition. Speed wins." Mike Marchev

10. TGIT: Thank Goodness It's Today!

Today, I am going to take a little poetic license and do something I have never done in any of my columns.

Everybody knows what the letters TGIF stand for, so I won't insult you with an explanation. For many years my four-letter reminder is **TGIT**. These four letters stand for **Thank Goodness Its Today.** Waiting to celebrate life until **Friday** arrives is a losing strategy. *There I said it.*

The word Friday is just another way to identify one of seven precious weekly time periods we have in each of our very short lives. Time waits for nobody, and "today" is the day we have been waiting for. You can be certain of this: Yesterday is a memory and tomorrow may or may not materialize. *Make today count.*

I want to direct you to a project I am working on with a client of mine. It involves producing a weekly **Podcast**. This is an audio format for sharing useful information with people who are receptive to new ideas, tactics, strategies and experiences. My program is titled **Mike'd Up Marchev** and is now listed on Spotify, iTunes, Google Podcasts, Travmarketmedia and soon to be other outlets. Take a listen and let me know what you think. Your creativity is bound to become stimulated.

https://www.travmarketmedia.com/author/mikemarchev/

The following falls under the topic of Market Research. I also have been writing a weekly column for nearly five years. Now that I think of it, I might be the original recipient of the affectionate title of "Wind Bag." If you are reading this book right now (and you are reading this chapter right now) send me a quick, short, painless email so I know somebody out there is reading my "stuff." mike@mikemarchev.com

You would be surprised how much a little input means to people. Let's expand on this thought. Starting tomorrow, if you are really serious about building your business, respond to those in your universe who are capturing your attention. Applaud their efforts and when appropriate, acknowledge their contributions to your life.

The sad truth is that very few people take the time to acknowledge superior behavior. The upside to this simple courtesy is ENORMOUS. (HUGE!)

Recap: (1) Take advantage of every single day. (2) Adopt **TGIT** as your new mantra. (3) Listen and subscribe to my new podcast to become and remain stimulated weekly. (4) Take time to professionally respond to people.

> Yesterday is a memory and tomorrow may or may not materialize.
>
> *Make today count.*

11. Sometimes Things Actually Do Work

My nephew and his girlfriend came to visit us this weekend from Brattleboro, VT. Andrew is my sister's son, and we were looking forward to meeting his new friend.

The Marchev family consists of a large group of fun-loving people who spend a major portion of their time together laughing and kidding each other mercilessly. I am very pleased to report that Sarah impressed us and proved to be capable and willing to go "toe-to-toe" with us.

But that is not the theme of tonight's story. Andrew and Sarah met online. Yes. Through a dating App. Sometimes things actually do work.

If these two never rolled the dice, chances are they would have never found each other. They took a shot. It appears it was a winning shot. I venture to say, although I have no direct experience in this field, that most dating App acquaintances do not work.

How does this budding relationship relate to your business? I think the correlation should be obvious. Borrowing a quote from the great Wayne Gretzky of NHL Hockey fame, **"You miss 100% of the shots you don't take."**

I am sure about one thing as it pertains to your business. If you don't take the appropriate steps in the right direction, not much good can come from your inactivity. Perhaps it is time that you take a risk in favor of your future. Maybe you could step out of your comfort zone for a minute or two and try something totally out of character. Who knows? Your "shot in the dark" just might hit the mark. Someone once reminded us that even a blind squirrel finds a nut now and then.

Andrew found Sarah on a whim. Sarah found Andrew because she rolled the dice.

Sometimes things do work.

In the interest of time, I chose not to bore you with a few of my successes that came about as a result of my taking a chance. My many failures would probably prove more entertaining, but I will leave those for another day. As for now, let it suffice to say, tomorrow is another day. It is another perfect day to **"Go roll the bones."**

"Go roll the bones" = Roll the dice.

12. Stop. Think. Act.

This is perhaps the sagest advice I could give you as another day ends with hope for a better tomorrow. I am borrowing this title from another three-word reminder we are all familiar with when it comes to railroad crossings: ***STOP-LOOK-LISTEN.***

Every 24-hours, when I find myself preparing for another night of restless sleep, I reflect on how time is passing without my permission. I am not sure where the finish line is or when I will be crossing it, but I do know I have a finite number of miles to cover before my race is over.

What better time to remind you that lamenting about today's mistakes or down-and-out failures is not the most prudent way to spend the precious minutes left on your dance card. And as Fleetwood Mac sings so eloquently in song, **"Don't stop thinking about tomorrow. Don't stop. It will soon be here."**

Another tomorrow will soon be here. Put the Dow Jones, Covid-19, your personal political opinions, and the opinions of others aside for a moment.

STOP. Simon and Garfunkel said it best when they reminded us to, "Slow down. You're moving too fast. You've got to make the morning last." Smell the roses. Notice the cloud formations. Actually, taste your food tomorrow. Take a walk. Call a friend. Live in the moment.

THINK. How can you add meaningful value to the lives of others? What can you do that will make a few of your close friends, associates and clients glad they know you?

ACT. Review your current "To-Do List" and take a step forward. If you are not sure what to do, do something. Your actions will be responsible for your future results. Act.

And I suppose there is a fourth step you can insert here.

OBSERVE. Pay attention to your current actions and how you spend your day. Notice what is working and what may be holding you back. Identify the pros and cons in your life. Make any required corrections and continue your journey forward. The pat you take is entirely up to you.

I wonder! "Will your tomorrow be better than your today based on today's four-word action plan? **STOP - THINK - ACT - OBSERVE.**

*****Based on my observations and years of experience, I am afraid that most of your tomorrows will unfold exactly like most of your yesterdays. *Please prove me wrong.*

13. It Isn't Over Until It Is Over

I believe we give credit to the Yankee catcher Yogi Berra for this pivotal reminder. "It ain't over until it is over." An off shoot of this sometimes refers to an over-weight soprano singing the lyrics to God Bless America. ("It isn't over until the fat lady sings.") Note: **The phrase is generally understood to be a reference to opera sopranos, who were typically heavyset and close the show.**

According to the latest news reports, summer is now over since Labor Day has come and gone. And although many people are beginning to act like Covid-19 is over, even without an advanced medical degree, I can assure you that it isn't. But there is something more important than both of these examples that is not over yet. *YOU.*

You are not over yet. You are not done yet building, pursuing, enjoying, creating, caring, loving, crying, laughing and living.

The sad truth is that many people today are walking around like it is over for them. It appears they have "given up the ghost" and are just meandering through the rest of their years.

SNAP OUT OF IT. (As Cher clearly pointed out to Nicholas Cage in the movie Moonstruck.)

At the expense of sounding like a broken record I will gently remind you that there is a lot more work to be done. By both you and me. Let the naysayers ply their trade. Let the macho groups insist on swimming against the tide. Let the "suits" schedule their meetings. Not you. Not me.

There are people out there who need us (Not everybody.) You are not "over" yet and the fat lady has not even started to sing.

It isn't over until it is over.

14. Your Tone Speaks Volumes

Someone once told me that elephants don't bite. Mosquitoes do. This is a clever way of reminding us that it is the little things that annoy us the most.

I was reminded of this when a former business acquaintance "reached out" and gave me an unexpected phone call. It had been a while since we last spoke which was a result of two busy people trying to make ends meet. It was good to hear his voice again.

In a few short minutes I detected uneasiness in his voice. I did not mention it at first as we were too busy catching up. Detecting a momentary break in the flow of the conversation, I couldn't help myself. I asked him point blank what was bothering him since his tone was a dead giveaway that something wasn't right.

He responded as one would predict, "Nothing's wrong. Why do you ask?"

"It sounds like you have 400 pounds of dead weight on your shoulders" I said. "Are you sure you are okay?"

I'll leave the story there for now. Hopefully, my point has been made. When calling people on the phone, the only thing you have going for you is your voice. Since I can't see you or interpret your body language, I must rely on your word choice, tone and inflection to fully interpret your message. Your voice has to carry the load. And although there might have been nothing wrong with my business friend, this man's voice painted a totally different picture.

The issue was that my attention drifted from his message to my apparently false interpretation. This is how it works. And this is what you must try to avoid. It is in your best interest to come across on all phone communications as the upbeat, happening person you are. You can't allow a little laziness to sabotage your business relationships. Your clients have too many other options for buying travel once they interpret you as somebody who is not absolutely delighted to be speaking with them.

We all have our personal issues, problems and concerns. I am fully involved with mine and quite frankly, I don't have the time or the interest in adopting yours as my own.

As a general rule, people like to be around people who are "upbeat and positive." With this in mind, here are my suggestions:

1. **Be cognizant of your "tone" when speaking**. What you are thinking may not be what others are hearing.
2. **When feeling a little funky, stay off the phone**. (If you do answer it, you better be good at pretending that you are feeling good.) It does not take much to destroy the goodwill you have been building for years.

3. **Remember that 100% of your marketing dollars are spent for the single purpose of having someone contact you.** When your phone rings, don't jeopardize your future by sounding like you are carrying the weight of the world on your shoulders.

Tone is an essential element in the marketing mix. Make sure that your tone is working for you and not against you.

15. You Market for Tomorrow

The following is not an isolated case. Your business is running along like a fine Swiss watch when out of the blue comes some unexpected input that sets you back on your heels. It could be a mechanical failure, a force of nature, a change in personnel or a runaway virus. Regardless of the source, your wheels of progress are suddenly derailed.

I was introduced to an unfortunate situation earlier today and the solution, albeit a tad too late, was obvious. The company in question had been riding favorable winds when all of a sudden it became apparent that they would soon be in for some tough sledding.

Yesterday there was no need to market their services as their plates were full and the future looked rosy. Today however, a lack of business caused a great deal of stress with knee-jerk ideas of how to calm the storm.

When your back is to the wall the chances of a short-term favorable outcome are slim at best. Introductions take time. Relationships take time. Business takes time. As the old saying goes, "the best time to grow a tree was twenty years ago." The best time to safeguard your future was weeks, months and years ago.

Marketing can be thought of as "setting the table." And as we all know, setting a table comes long before sitting down and enjoying the meal. So, without exploring the many options of positioning yourself in your personal marketplace, I will leave you with the following thought:

Avoid stop-and-go marketing practices. Stay consistent. Be persistent. Remain visible.

16. You Didn't Get This Far by Accident!

You did not get this far by some quirk of fate. Granted, today's challenges may be unprecedented, but challenges of any shape and size are not new. We have come a long way since our first birthday, and we have always managed to overcome what seemed at the time to be insurmountable obstacles. Tomorrow is no different. You shall prevail.

I suppose my message today can be summed up by reminding you that **"What doesn't kill you makes you stronger."**

The travel industry does not corner the market on this statement, as we both know that *plenty of stuff happens in our business,* and some *stuff* can be filed in the *"Why Me?"* folder.

Some stuff is down-right devastating, while other stuff just slides off your back. Some stuff stings while other stuff makes you laugh and scratch your head in amusement. **Bottom line: Stuff happens.**

Nobody ever implied that life would or should be fair. Nobody said that your business is going to be hassle-free simply because you are one of the good guys. In fact, that is *why* you are in business... to help your clients get over, through and around the rough spots.

Nobody is as good as you are when it comes to the phrase **"When the going gets tough, the tough get going."**

You did not get this far in life by accident. Who you are today is the sum total of everything you have experienced along the way...both good and bad.

The result? You're okay. You are better than okay. You are good. You are <u>*very*</u> good.

17. The Importance of Leading a Disciplined Life

"**Success is about doing the right thing, not about doing everything right. The secret to success is to choose the right habit and bring just enough discipline to establish it.**"

The above quote is from Gary Keller and it is shared in his book titled *The One Thing*.

For years I have been asked to share my thoughts on **Time Management**. It is a popular theme and one that would draw huge crowds to a seminar room. Unfortunately, I am not qualified to offer any salient points on this subject. Reason being is that "time" does not require management. *YOU DO.*

The plight of today's travel advisor is the feeling they have to do everything themselves. Heaven knows there is not a shortage of "to-do's." The truth of the matter is there isn't enough time in a day to get it all done. There is too much to do and not enough time to do it.

This has the earmarks of a true conundrum. But the sad fact is you have all the time there is, and you can't possibly do it all yourself... nor do you *have* to.

Back in 1896 The Pareto Principle came to light. It reminded us that 80% of our results come from 20% of our efforts. Inversely, this implies that much of our time is wasted on tasks of little or no significance. I have a solution, and you can be sure it is easier to read than to implement.

In order to W.I.N. you must determine **What's Important Now**. That is the premise of Mr. Keller's book. On every to-do list, regardless of the number of tasks listed, there is just one item that represents "*THE*" one thing.

I realize that it would be easy to address tasks 1, 3, 6, 12, and 22 on your list of things to do and cross off all five thinking you are one efficient time machine. You would feel that you have this time management thing down to a science. That would really make you feel like you are "cooking with gas."

Regardless of the length of your list however, there is always a single entry (the "one thing") that deserves (and requires) your focused attention. The key is to concentrate on that "one thing" until it is completed to your satisfaction, or you arrive at a logical stopping point. Only then is it time to turn your attention to the next "one thing."

It takes discipline to switch from quantity to quality. Starting tomorrow, identify your "one thing" on your list and you will soon see that discipline will take care of your time management.

18. Take Responsibility for Your Future.

Author David McNally went on record to say, **"It seems there is no tougher challenge than to accept personal responsibility for who we are, and who we can become."**

When I read this quote, I immediately remembered another line from the movie producer Woody Allen. The Woodster said he **"had accomplished many fine things in his life, but he managed to come up short on a number of occasions. What he did not accomplish was his own fault.**

I have been sharing this quote with audiences for nearly 30 years. It is what I refer to as a **"Keeper."** Mr. Allen was given numerous opportunities to do more with his life, but according to him, he can't blame his failures on anybody but himself.

And so it is with your business. Since you do not have to place a large investment in inventory or raw materials, you have the ideal business model to succeed. You have equal access to the planes, ships, hotels, and destinations that are available to everyone. You have equal access to a market approaching 8 billion people and access to the required technology.

To accomplish your wildest dreams, all you need to do is decide if you are willing to pay the price in time and effort to

(1) become visible and (2) to introduce your service to a handful of those nearly 8 billion people.

If for some reason you do not succeed to the level you had in mind, chances are it is nobody's fault but your own.

Fact: You are who you are.
Fact: You can be what you want to become.
Fact: You must decide to pay the price.
Fact: The ball is in your court.

19. Multitasking Is a Game for Losers

"Losers" may be too strong a word, but if it caught your attention I'll stick with it. There probably is a milder word, but the subject of today's article is "**Multitasking**."

In a previous story" I quoted author Gary Keller with a reference to his book titled ***The One Thing***. Today I want to share a second quote from the same author.

"With research overwhelmingly clear, it seems insane that – knowing how multitasking leads to mistakes, poor choices, and stress – we attempt it anyway."

This topic has more flammability than a recent presidential debate. People in the travel industry (and in all industries for that matter) feel incredibly overwhelmed. They feel a necessity to keep a number of "balls in the air." My advice is to leave the juggling to the circus clowns. They get paid to juggle with no downside if they fail.

I have heard all your excuses and all ten thousand reasons why working on multiple assignments comes with the territory. Not unlike everybody else in this business you have lots on your plate and lots more riding on your effectiveness. You also can go excuse for excuse with the best of them.

That being said, I maintain my stance that the only person who benefits from multiple activity proceedings is ... nobody.

My personal definition of multitasking is **"the ability to screw up a number of jobs all at the same time."** Nobody wins. Numerous people become upset. You take one more step toward the Looney-Bin, and worse yet, you risk losing your credibility and the confidence of your valued clients as your work resembles mediocrity.

"Focus" is the word of the day, week, month and year. Focus is what it takes to avoid mistakes. Focus leads to making good choices while minimizing your debilitating stress quotient.

My advice to you is to leave the practice of multitasking to the amateurs. Take one focused step at a time. Work on one itinerary at a time. Slow down. Do the right things right. Become more efficient. Make more money. Stay in business. Smile more. Be happy.

PS: The truth is you can do more than one thing at once. You can iron a shirt while listening to the radio. But what you can't do is **focus** on more than one thing at a time. I rest my case.

20. A Gentle "Wake Up Call" Might Be in Order

Regardless of how many years you have been in business and how experienced you may be, a periodic **"Wake up Call"** is sure to come your way. And it just may be exactly what you need. My most recent "wake-up call" came last week when I was asked to edit a client's Special Lead Generating Report.

The report in question was excellently written. Other than a few grammatical errors my contributions were incidental. That was not the "call" I am talking about. It came soon after the travel advisor shared his marketing strategy with me that I once again, "saw the light."

Here is today's thought.

The agent in this story is measurably successful by anyone's definition. He sells both high and low-ticket items and has an envious referral record. In short, his business is humming along nicely.

But this seasoned professional understands how the game of business works. Today's good news is more often than not the result of a whole bunch of smart work performed in days past. One must continue "seeding and fertilizing" if tomorrow's crop is going to be worth harvesting.

But in his case, he was wise enough to know that "a bird in the hand is worth two in the bush." Although he was writing a lead generating special report, he did not want to take any of his current clients for granted. He understood what "first things first" actually meant. He had to solidify the current relationships he had with all his clients before setting out to acquire a new batch of customers. **And here comes the "wake-up call."**

His plan of action was to grab the attention and initial interest of just five to seven new prospects a month. This would leave him enough time to care for his current clients and still find time to follow up with his new batch of clients. Of those people indicating an interest in his special report, he would try to turn two into paying clients. In review: One Special Report – Five people raising their hand – two new clients.

BRILLIANT! This is very manageable. This is very realistic. This is very logical. This is very doable. This is very profitable.

The lesson here is two-fold.

#1. Take care of your current customer list first.

#2. Create a future lead generating plan that can be implemented day in and day out without you having to remortgage your house or give yourself a mild case of agita.

Before: Take care of your current client list.

After: Implement a slow, manageable lead generation campaign.

21. Clarity of Intention

This next quote from an unknown author caught my attention. Why? Perhaps it was because I have always been a practitioner of the *Shiny Bauble Syndrome*.

 "**Clarity of intention launched with enthusiasm is the most potent combination known to humankind. It is the basis of all accomplishment.**" **Author Unknown**

Wanting to grow your business is admirable. Wishing for more profitable sales is a worthwhile objective. Hoping things work out for you in the long run should come as no surprise. Praying for the strength to do what is right is admirable.

The hard truth is that you must do something if you want to see progress. **Wanting, wishing, hoping and praying are not enough.** But doing just anything is not the answer either. Although doing anything might be better than doing nothing, it will prove to be time ill-spent if you do not do the right things right.

If you are one of the many who still believe that selling is a numbers game you may be in for some hard times. Tossing enough "stuff" against a wall may result in some sticking, but it definitely is not the shortest or surest route to a larger bank account.

As soon as you see the light and compare the art of selling to a "game of darts" you will begin to add some girth to your bank account. (Reread chapter 5, page 14.)

Clarity of intention when speaking of sales, implies that you have an unwavering idea (picture) of your targeted prospect. You know who they are by name and exactly what their needs are. You know what they look like, sound like, think like and you know the actions required to stimulate meaningful forward progress.

Then, with thanks going to your self-esteem and personal confidence quotient, you can show your selected audience how exciting the wonderful the world of travel can be, and how you can help them enjoy the ride.

Your success will not arrive by accident. It will be directly proportional to your *clarity of intention*.

22. Are You "Laughing & Scratching" Regularly?

I was speaking with my brother the other day when he asked me if I ever began laughing out loud while driving down the road thinking how lucky we are? I said I knew exactly what he was talking about. As far as I am concerned, COVID or no COVID, political embarrassment or not, overall, I am generally pleased with my life.

Right, wrong or indifferent, for the first sixty-five plus years, I spent a lot of time "laughing and scratching" down the road based on the philosophy, **"Good enough is good enough."**

When I hit age 65, and for the next ten years, I began questioning this philosophy. Looking back over my life I started to think that maybe I should have spent a little more time pursuing excellence. Perhaps if I did, I would still be "laughing and scratching" .... but on a higher level.

Then I read this passage, and I began to ease off the accelerator.

"Perfectionism is a self-protective mechanism that prevents us from flourishing through our vulnerability. It is particularly pervasive in professional contexts. Perfectionism isn't the pursuit of excellence, nor is it about

self-improvement. It's really about attempting to win approval, where one's sense of self-worth is reliant on external measures of success. The sooner we let it go, the sooner we can start finding the courage to succeed and lead on our own terms."

Maybe being good enough is good enough after all. I know my "good enough" could have been a little better at times. But maybe we all just need to lighten up and spend a little more time just being us.

I've said this before. In all likelihood, you did not get this far by accident. Today, tomorrow and for the rest of the year, keep doing what you are doing with your own personal flair. If nothing else, you just might find yourself "laughing and scratching" until you too break into laughter while driving down the road reflecting on just how happy you are being you.

PS. Find more reasons to laugh...and perhaps a few less reasons to scratch.

23. Stop Worrying and Just Hit the Ball

It seems like just yesterday when I found myself browsing through my TV channels when I arrived at The US Open Golf Tournament. I remember saying to myself, "It is a shame there are no spectators," I watched an unknown golfer putt his ball and watch it travel 28 feet before disappearing into the cup.

My mind shot back to a book I read by Bob Rotella titled **"Putting Out of Your Mind."** I flashed back to a passage that read, **"Your problem is that you're worrying about speed instead of putting to make it."**

Let's think about this.

The golf ball is not moving. It is still and it is right in front of you. The hole is off in the distance, but you can see it from where you are standing. All you have to do is take aim at the hole and strike the ball in the direction of the target with the stick you are holding. How hard can it be?

But as we both know it is not that easy. Your mind clicks in and all sorts of information begins to pass through your head like a run-away horse on a mission. "Do this. Remember that. Not too far left. Not too hard. How is my stance? My grip? Should I remove my glove or tighten it? What kind of grass is this? Am I detecting a slight fall-off toward the river? If I miss, can I keep the ball below the hole." Yada, yada, yada. This is often referred to as mindless chatter which is the precursor of the "yips."

Message: Stop worrying. There are only two types of putt: Putts that drop into the hole, and putts that don't. What are you waiting for? Take a read. Make a decision. Hit the ball. You will find out soon enough which type of putt you just hit.

I'll say it again. Do the appropriate due diligence, do your homework, analyze the options and then "pull the trigger." I am sort of implying that you adopt the philosophy, "READY – FIRE – AIM. (But with a modicum of preparation.)

24. A Lesson from Your Morning Crossword Puzzle

Something has been on my mind for days and I am finally going to get it off my chest. It involves the connection between a daily crossword puzzle and running a successful travel business. (Yes, as we age the mind works in funny ways.)

A few years back I was introduced to the online version of USA Today's Crossword Puzzle. It is the same one that appears in the daily newspaper edition. This was a new experience for me and in the beginning, I found it very difficult to arrive at the correct solution for each clue. As a result, I opted for the "regular" version that notifies me immediately if I am making a mistake with red lettering.

I have noticed a few interesting occurrences over the years as I muddle through the clues. I will read a clue and have absolutely no idea of the answer. I will turn to another clue and immediately know the correct answer. The first letter of my correct answer was all that I needed to steer my thinking in the right direction to figure out the answer of the clue I previously had no answer for. (Did you follow that line of thinking?)

Sometimes I need two letters to solve the temporary conundrum. And on I go each and every morning, letter-by-letter, word-by-word until I smile with satisfaction knowing that I single-handedly accomplished another formidable "life-changing" task.

And so it is with our businesses. We are presented with challenges each day that tax our knowledge and creativity. We appear lost until we receive a clue in the form of some additional information. Then as if by magic, we arrive at the correct solution and life goes on as planned.

When you hit a roadblock in your business, think of it as an unknown puzzle clue. Don't quit. Investigate other clues that are more familiar to you. I am betting that the link (or chain) will soon become obvious and before you know it, you will be back on top of your game.

I realize this story might appear a bit out in "left field" to you, but it made perfect sense to me.

Look for the clues that will lead you to more solutions. When you find yourself totally stumped, move onto the next project, challenge or next step in the process. More often than not, as if by magic, you will find yourself arriving at the correct answer.

25. Read That Book Again

It dawned on me recently that a well-accepted objective is to finish the book you start. More often than not, or primary mission is to get to the end of the book. When you stop to think about it this behavior is counterproductive. Let me see if I can explain my position.

You buy a book, or you are told to read one in school. The first thing you do is turn to the Table of Contents to see what lies in store for you. You might also flip to the back to see what kind of investment you are about to make timewise as you see this baby has 465 pages of ink. To make matters worse, the font is Times Roman in 10-point type. Yuk!

You begin your journey. and you soon find yourself seeking logical stopping points. For many this is at a chapter's conclusion. For others it is on any page that ends with a period.

You are making good progress. You are already on page 265 and you are either heavily engrossed in the plot by now or you have learned a few new skills. You have only 200 pages to go. "I can knock this baby off in no time" you say to yourself as you turn off the light and adjust your pillow.

On the other hand, doesn't it make sense to slow your reading down in order to grasp each nuance as it appears in print? Picture the passing scenery and envision the budding relationship in the making. Stop worrying about "finishing" and spend more time comprehending and retaining important concepts. Who cares if you only manage to digest 5-6 pages per sitting? Your goal is not to "finish." Your goal is to think, concentrate, focus, interpret, analyze, digest, recall and learn.

Here is a novel idea. If you find a book you thoroughly enjoyed reading, (fact or fiction) read it a second time. The messages and enjoyment received the second time around will be just as exciting ... if not more so. As you grow as an individual, your interpretations change to fit your current surroundings. Read it again.

In review: Don't read for speed. Read to comprehend while enhancing your skill level and expanding your knowledge base.

26. Crossword Puzzles and Books

In the last chapter I shared my thoughts on speed reading verses focused comprehension. I will now shift to another daily practice that in many cases results in wasted opportunities.

As you now know, I begin each day by filling out USA Today's Online Crossword Puzzle. It dawned on me the other day that I was wasting an opportunity to enhance my general knowledge base in an effort to "complete" the puzzle.

Let me explain.

There are many clues that result with instant recall. You understand the clue and you immediately know the word. There are other clues that have you flummoxed right from the giddy-up. You have absolutely no idea what the answer could be. But with the help of the first letter, or perhaps a letter or two within the answer, your mind shifts into gear and "voila," you solve the line item.

You continue finding that many answers are filled in by simply addressing other clues. This is where the missed opportunity presents itself. You find yourself striving to complete the puzzle of the day by hook or by crook. You don't bother to digest the fact that the name of the author in five-down was a new piece of information. (In many cases you really couldn't care less who wrote XYZ back in 1845.) But my point is valid.

There is a bunch of new information presented each morning and without pausing long enough to internalize this input, your knowledge base will remain the same. You already know what you already know. The idea is to build upon your base of knowledge, little by little each and every morning by being introduced to new information.

Here is what I suggest. After completing the puzzle in your normal fashion, erase the entries and play it again. This time focus on each and every clue and think about each and every answer. Pause. Think. Internalize.

When I do this, the second pass through usually takes just minutes to complete. But by doing so, I retain a whole bunch of new knowledge.

I realize I may be preaching to the puzzle choir today, but as in most of my stories, I find myself writing to me. And heaven forbid, if you happen to be wired like I am, this story just might give you something to think about.

27. Don't Stop Thinking About Tomorrow

I am not wearing my "feel-good" hat today thinking I could make the world a better place by putting "lipstick on a pig." We are all currently facing the most challenging times of our lives. Make no mistake about it. We have been, and will continue to be, in for some challenging times.

But that being said, this is the hand we have been dealt. Our only recourse is to play our cards accordingly. What other options do we have?

It comes as no surprise to see some people walking around looking as if they have just lost their best friend. These people are clearly communicating that life is, and will continue to be, an unfair experience. Daily existence is a total drag for them while life offers nothing in return for their "showing up." If you know one or more of these individuals (and I'm betting you do) let me remind you that trying to improve the future of anyone engaged in an exercise in self-pity is an exercise in futility. You just aren't that good ... or talented.

Don't think for a moment that it is your responsibility to get these people singing happy songs. (It isn't going to happen.) Your job is to get *your* thinking straight, in step and positive so that you can significantly contribute to those anticipating a productive existence.

Here is today's phrase that pays:

*You can't change the world... but you can change **your** world.*

Your job is to energize yourself while making certain you don't get confused for the walking dead. Once you take care of you, your actions will do the talking. People are attracted to those who are alive, energetic, upbeat and happy – who have ideas and exciting plans for life – and who have kind things to say about others.

I love the Fleetwood Mac song phrase that reminds us to, **"Don't stop thinking about tomorrow. Don't stop, it will soon be here. It will soon be here ... better than before."**

So, if you truly want to become the exception, pick a game... any game... and get into the game with both feet. Become a positive player. **Never stop thinking about tomorrow.**

28. Elephants Don't Bite

In a "me-too-only-cheaper" competitive, environment, strict adherence to the details (the little things) will position you faster and more accurately than just about anything else.

Take these three facts...

• **Fact**: Customers are in the driver's seat.
• **Fact**: Customers have a number of options when preparing to make a purchase– and they know what they are.
• **Fact**: Your success has everything to do with how you manage the "little things."

It is true that it takes many months to find a new account but only one goof-up to lose one. It makes sense then to pay attention to the **details** when it comes to dealing with prospects and customers.

Solidify the relationship you have with your base of accounts by making them glad they have selected you as their travel professional. Since the smallest error, mistake, misinterpretation or oversight could blow your previous track record out of the water (and set your company back a couple of months) focus on every little task at hand. Dot those i's... cross those t's ... and think "details."

Each and every employee must pull his or her weight. "Each" is spelled **(E-V-E-R-Y-O- N-E)**. Avoid shooting yourself in the foot and losing what you already earned for some foolish reason, or as a result of opting for a shortcut.

Here is a reminder for you. **NEVER** take a valued customer for granted. Pay attention to them especially when they **DON'T** have anything on the books.

Now is the time to prove your value and worth to your current client base. You can do this by simply doing what you say you will do... the right way ... each and every time. Overlooking or ignoring the little things will put some major hurt in your life and it does not have to happen.

It is usually not the big items that will hurt you. It is the little things. Said another way, **Elephants don't bite. Mosquitoes do**.

29. Failure Is Not Something to Avoid

Mistakes are good things. They are not something you strive to make, but they are not something you want to shy away from. The word mistake is synonymous with the word failure and failing remains your fastest path to success. There, I said it again.

Think back to when you first mounted your two-wheel ride. (Bike) You did not master the concept the first time you saddled up. Somebody, (probably one of your parents) urged you to continue pedaling after you skinned your knee once or twice trying to find your balance. (If at first you don't succeed, try, try again.)

Then one day as if by magic, you began to roll. From that day forward it became impossible to lose your balance. Riding your bike became second nature.

Learning to ride your bike was hard enough. Learning how to turn a profit in your business today is a more formidable challenge. But it is not as hard as you may be making it. All you need to do is initiate a proven formula, and then learn something new each time you screw something up.

"Don't be silly, Mike," I can hear many of you saying. "Our job is to succeed; not fail." I agree. But doesn't it make sense to succeed as fast as you can? By design? Of course it does. His where "failure" enters the picture.

The secret is to become experienced. And as hard as you wish, hope, and pray, experience does not come without a price. It is the result of a great deal of consistent, focused action directed toward a worthwhile objective.

And here is a bonus idea for you. Once you get your "ducks in a row" and understand the steps needed to be taken, your efforts will begin to take on a life of their own. You will find that you will be enjoying the learning process more since you won't be beating yourself up every time you come up short.

Here is an analogy. The hardest thing in sport according to me, is hitting a baseball traveling at 95 mph with a rotation causing it to change direction on its way to the plate. The very best in baseball fail to hit the ball safely seven out of ten times. A .300 batting percentage ranks among the league's best. I am just as quick to suggest that running a successful business today is just as difficult as winning the batting title.

Message: Continue to gain experience by making more mistakes. Keep swinging. Fail faster. Fail more often. Fail with a purpose, but always fail while keeping your eye on the "target." The hits will come. The sales will come. The joy will return.

30. I Love It When a Plan Comes Together

One of the many truths I have learned during my 72 years of dancing and scratching my way to this point in life is that everything has a flip side. I mean EVERYTHING. To give you just one example: "Haste makes waste," is a phrase we all can come to grips with. But soon we are reminded, "He who hesitates is lost." Total opposite message.

Recently I was confronted with a situation where I had to decide if the fall was a good time to plant a little grass, or should I wait until springtime. I Googled the quandary and was soon confronted with two opposing opinions. One response suggested spring was the ideal time to green-up your front yard while another endorsed the cooler autumn weather. This is what is known in the horticultural arena as a "real conundrum."

I decided to cast my fate to the wind and before I knew it I was preparing my designated plot with a mixture of topsoil and seasoned goat manure. The month was September, and the first frost had come and gone.

I'm sharing this story with you for a couple of reasons. First, you will be inundated with opposing recommendations as you pursue a successful career. There never seems to be one correct answer. Pick one. As they teach us in golf, line up your putt, make a decision as to its projected roll, and hit the thing. If it does not drop into the hole, hit it again.

In my case, I Googled. I read and I made a decision. I tossed a billion seeds into the prepared ground.

(To tie this back to business: I researched. I made a plan. I did something.)

Stay with me. This will all make sense in a minute or two. I knew that a billion seeds would not result in a billion blades of grass. But regardless of the outcome I knew my efforts to this point would all be in vain if I did not follow through with some focused attention. A regular watering routine was now in order. I began to water daily only to see... nothing happen. I kept on watering. Still nothing.

Then one day as if by magic I spotted something that appeared to be a single blade of grass. It was green and it stuck straight up in the air. After focusing for a minute my eye caught a second blade. Then a third. My plan was working. I was growing grass. My efforts were paying dividends. I was a horticultural genius. (Horticulturalist may be the wrong word. Maybe Landscaper Extraordinaire paints a more accurate picture.) Whatever you call it, I was in my element.

Let me net this thing out in the interest of time so I can go outside and continue watering my budding lawn. (1) You must prepare the groundwork; (2) You must toss plenty of seeds knowing most will not germinate; (3) You must follow through and continue to manage your project; (4) You must keep on keeping on once you begin to see results.

As foolish as it may sound, I was genuinely excited when I saw my efforts paying noticeable dividends. My grass was actually taking root. I would have probably experienced the same results if I waited for the spring, but now I will be mowing my new project in May rather than still "thinking" about it.

Begin planting your seeds tomorrow and start watering them like your future depends on it.

31. You Can't Tell a Book by Its Cover

I woke earlier than usual this morning to stoke the fire, make some coffee and begin browsing through a few recorded TED videos. One of the more popular ones was only nine minutes long. Most TED videos are between 18-20 minutes in length. Short, sweet, and on point. I clicked on the nine-minute speech and was soon watching a young bathing suit model talking about self-image. (This woman was not the most polished speaker I have reviewed, but I immediately appreciated why this was one of the more popular TED videos.)

Although it would be highly entertaining, I won't bore you with the details of her presentation. I will, however, share the major take-away. This young lady was tall, slim and more than slightly attractive. Her message was that her success had a lot to do with her clothes, hair stylist, make-up artist, pre and postproduction professionals and more than a tad of re-touching of photos. She went on to say that although her highly polished appearance drew initial attention, nobody knew her for who she really was. She was a true to life example of the saying, *"looks are not everything."*

She shared her observation that in the majority of cases "models" are lacking self-esteem and inner confidence. She reminded her audience that many (most) people spend the majority of their waking hours seeking an appearance beyond their current reality. Example: Taller; shorter; shinier hair; thicker hair; longer legs; slimmer waist; fuller lips; higher cheek bones, etc. They feel success lies in obtaining the "have-nots."

I personally interpreted her message as the importance of projecting the authentic you. Be who you are. Use what you have and know that even though you can alter your appearance, you will remain exactly who you are. And the people who count will appreciate you for who you are and not for what you look like.

I am not suggesting that you adopt a lazy, sloppy "what-you-see-is-what-you-get" attitude. A clean outward appearance with clothes that match more often than not won't do you any harm. A haircut now and then might also be in your best interest. Just don't go overboard spending too much time wondering, "why can't I be more like him/her?"

**** I know I have not done justice to this message. I can hear some of you saying, "That is easy for a model to say." Here is the link to the TED Video titled "Looks Are Not Everything" by Cameron Russell
https://www.youtube.com/watch?v=KM4Xe6DIp0Y44

32. The Next One Could Be the Big One

I was recently reviewing a few archived Inner Circle sales meetings and I came across the following soundbite: It was Thomas Edison who said, **"It is a shame to see many (if not most) people quit just one experiment short of finding the solution."**

This single sentence had my mind spinning with past phrases, suggestions, recommendations and reminders of mine with regard to the concept of quitting too soon.

One particular reminder came to mind. **"The next one could be the big one."** What does this mean? It implies that we do not know what the "next opportunity" will look like, sound like, smell like or taste like. We do not know if the "next one" will be the next phone call that will change our lives. Or the next email. Or the next introduction. Or the next sales letter. Or the next proposal. Or the next request for a referral. Or the next anything.

In baseball, the next pitch could be the one that meets the sweet spot of the bat and CRACK ... another run (or four) for the good guys. Remember this: **"The next one could be the BIG one."**

I would be remiss if I did not remind you that 50% of all sales professionals quit after a single attempt at making a sale. An additional 25% stop calling on prospects after a second try. And here comes the differentiating statistic. 80% of all sales happen *AFTER* multiple contacts (Five or more.) If this does not put a little wind in your sales or some **"MOJO"** in your selling efforts than I must be speaking to deaf ears.

Bottom Line(s): (1) Don't quit too soon and (2) Keep swinging.

The next one could be the BIG one.

33. Podcasts "R" Us

Many agents have asked if I thought podcasts are a good way to remain visible. The answer is an unqualified yes.... with a "but" ... and a "however."

Like everything else you have at your fingertips, podcasts can prove to be a lot of work. They can also be a huge waste of time if you do not produce a meaningful broadcast with lots of good information. It helps if you find an audience who takes the time to listen to your words, opinions, experiences and recommendations.

The upsides are numerous
(1) You will become more knowledgeable.
(2) You will become a better presenter.
(3) You will position yourself as a reliable resource.
(4) You will continue to build your relationship.
(5) You will have a tool to gain access to hard-to-reach people.

The possible downsides.
(1) You don't prepare properly and come across as unorganized.
(2) You present "fluff" and fail to grab the ongoing attention of your audience.
(3) You fail to gain traction by not podcasting on a regular basis.

Producing a podcast and promoting a podcast are two different animals. There are many books and YouTube videos available to help you get started. For now, you might want to subscribe and listen to a handful of other topic-related podcasts to give you a feel for what is currently being produced.

Go to www.TravMarketMedia.com and in addition to my podcast titled **Mike'd Up Marchev** you can listen to a few more travel-related podcasts.

34. Simple Is Better

One of my favorite all-time magazine covers was a cover for Business Week. The year was 1996. Proctor & Gamble suggested that **we make marketing simple.**

"Marketers sell too much stuff in too many different ways. Now the smart ones are cutting the complexity."

Whoever said "what was old is new again" had their hand on the pulse. With more and more people becoming more and more familiar with the workings of the Internet, we are all being inundated with marketing come-ons from all corners of the globe. (I bet you didn't know the globe had corners. Either did I.)

Letting people know what we do, how we do it, and why we do it while positioning us as the "good guys" has become a daunting task. At times, it seems it is approaching down-right impossible. Too many options. Too many people. Too much noise.

I've become oblivious to the **BOGO**'s offers. The **GUARANTEES**. The **FREE** initial consultations. **EXTENDED PAYMENT PLANS**. "**NO-RISK**" trial memberships. And the truth is that I have tried them all at one time or another with my marketing endeavors.

It is time we turn back the clock and take a hard look at P&G's Business Week Cover. What can you do to **MAKE IT SIMPLE?**

You can begin by being realistic. Understand your limitations and give a little more credit to your prospect's IQ. They know they have a plethora of options, and that you are not the only game in town. In many instances, they are more adept at working a computer and Googling for answers than you are. After all, they are FOCUSED on a single destination. Perhaps you would be better off seeing your clients as team members and not "target" audiences.

Next, you can give more than just lip-service to the notion that you can't be all things to all people. That was the error that P&G was focusing on. Take a bar of soap for example. There is no such thing anymore as a "bar of soap." Take a left down aisle five and you are confronted with no less than 200 choices of ways to wash your hands. (You don't believe me? Try buying some Tylenol. This exercise alone is enough to give you a headache.) Message: Make decision making easier. Narrow down your choices.

And finally, give your targeted audience what they are looking for and need most ... a person they can trust. Ask yourself, (1) Am I more interested in making a buck or in my client's total satisfaction? (2) Do I do what I say I'm going to do without exception or excuse? (3) Do I try to make all relationships with me fun, easy and simple?

Twenty-four years ago, P&G put it on the cover. I think it is time we all get the message. **Simple is better.**

35. Some Ideas Are Worth Repeating

Let me rephrase today's title. Some **GOOD** ideas are worth repeating.

A few stories back I shared my views on how a daily crossword puzzle can effectively remind us of the concept of leveraging information appropriately. While I fumbled through the USA Crossword Puzzle earlier this week the lesson resurfaced and I found myself smiling.

I don't say this very often, but this particular lesson is a "gem," and it is worth repeating. I will use slightly different words this time so as not to appear like a lazy slug by simply regurgitating my words from Story #24.

Same message. Different words. You read a clue sometimes and the answer immediately pops into mind. Twenty-two down, four letters. Clue: Popular shades of lipstick: REDS. Easy-peasy. At other times you read a clue and you literally do not have a clue. *Until you do.*

Six down. Six letters. Clue: Minor shortcoming. Nothing comes to mind. But once the four letters of six across are filled in and you see the first letter for six down is an "F" the word "**FOIBLE**" fits the bill. Voila! You cracked another one.

The same phenomenon is introduced in business on a daily basis. Some challenges resemble "a piece of cake," while others have us scratching our heads in bewilderment. When a clue pops into mind, and we look at the current conundrum from a slightly different angle ... from a new perspective ...the answer becomes obvious. When the answer or solution enters the picture, you are once again off and running.

I apologize if today's repeated message causes any degree of consternation on your part. But some things are worth repeating. When you get "stuck" in a business-related situation, don't stop looking for clues that you are in position to analyze. Chances are the ball will continue to bounce and before you realize what happened, you will be back in control whistling a happy tune.

36. There's No Such Thing As "Down-Time"

I am often asked where I get my ideas from for my marketing columns. My answer: *EVERYWHERE.*

I remember a warm fall afternoon when I was cooling my heels in a Honda Dealership in Yorkville, NY. There are some things that just don't have to happen with a little planning.... and discipline. (1) do not have to get a speeding ticket. (2) You do not have to run out of gas. (3) You do not have to own a car that does not operate as designed.

As a result, I service my car as the book suggests knowing I may be spending a tad more annually than needed. I just don't want to be bitten by #3 listed above.

Knowing what I do about car dealership reputations, I find myself lurking in a corner, masked up and paying attention to the service professionals as they pass through the sales department sharing a few lame jokes now and then. I have met many fine upstanding automotive professionals in my day, but by and large, I too approach them with a modicum of skepticism.

But that is not the topic of tonight's bedtime story. Utilizing "down-time" is what I want to address tonight. With time being our most precious commodity, it makes little sense to watch the secondhand sweep around the dial without our blessing. Yes, sometimes doing nothing is therapeutic and is exactly what the doctor ordered. (Sometimes.)

But with most of us dyed-in-wool entrepreneurs, down-time can be considered a blessing in disguise. Whether waiting for an oil change, a delayed flight to Chicago, a disturbingly late doctor keeping his appointment with you, or waiting for your significant other to aimlessly meander through the closest shopping mall, you have time to (1) review your latest proposal, (2) craft your next sales email, (3) draft an article you have been putting off, (4) return a phone call or two, (5) Google a series of potential group meeting locations, (6) delete outdated files from your laptop, (7) try your hand at USA Today's Crossword Puzzle, (8) outline the chapters of that book you have always wanted to publish ... and the list goes on.

With a modest dose of creativity, you too can eliminate the word "wasted time" from your vocabulary. Me? I am writing this reminder from the waiting room at Leadcar Honda in Yorkville. I am planning to write five more before I check my blood pressure later today after seeing my bill for today's work. (I was putting off buying a new pair of "shoes" for "Old Betsy" so four new tires just may put me over the edge. I wonder if there will be a future article in there somewhere. Time will tell.)

37. The Path to Success Is Usually Less Travelled

Whether you are a Jeopardy fan or not, the following statement is as true as rain. The definition of an "easy" question is one that you know the answer to. It should come as no surprise then to hear the definition of a hard question. That's right. It is a question you do not know the answer to.

With this as the basis for tonight's story I would like to share a strategy I consider to be both "easy" and logical. It may be my 72 years talking coupled to my many years of accumulating more misses than hits, but I believe growing a profitable business is easy. I also believe that you are making it a lot harder than it has to be.

I do not see what all the fuss is about. Who said that building a business had to be difficult? Certainly not me. Like everything worth pursuing, it is the fundamentals that will get you to where you're wanting to go.

In an attempt to simplify tonight's story, I've outlined five steps that will have you feeling like a pro in very short order. The work stems from the concept of "consistency," and not from tedious and laborious "work."

Let's break this down to its component parts.

(1) Identify a market consisting of people who want what you have/do. This may be a hard pill to swallow, but current cruisers are more attractive than the larger group who has never donned an orange jacket in a mandatory lifeboat drill.

(2) Introduce yourself to this identified market. No buckshot approach here. Determine exactly who you need to get to know. You will target them and position them on your "marketing dartboard."

(3) Qualify this group to make certain that what you have is what will "scratch their itch." There is no future in trying to force a square peg into a round hole. Your time is best spent speaking with people who want to talk to you.

(4) Make yourself visible and available. Make it easy for them to contact you. It is your job to maintain both visibility and availability. When they do contact you, pretend that you are actually pleased they called. (You should not have to pretend. This should not be an exercise in make-believe.) And I should not have to say this ... but I did...and I do.

In time, you will be given an opportunity to strut your stuff... to showcase your expertise... to earn your stripes... to *cash their checks.*

That's it. That is all you need to do, every day, with consistency, with personality, and with a sense of professionalism.

But if this is so easy, why aren't more people successful at sales? That is also an easy question to answer. Because most people fail to buy-in to this formula. They feel that their gift-of-gab will deliver them to the promised land. Or they feel that if they build a better mousetrap, the market will find its way to their door. This is outdated thinking. This is mindless thinking. "How so, Mike?" you ask.

The entry-demands for selling travel are simple. You don't have to buy anything. All you need to do is to learn to say, "me-too" and go print yourself a business card with a multi-colored fancy travel-related logo. Add a clever saying next to some clipart and include your email address and VOILA .... you are a sales professional.

The options all consumers have today are limitless. At last count, there were 25 bazillion ways to book a trip to Europe or a room with an ocean-view in Cancun. The fastest way to the poor house is to do what everybody else does when it comes to selling travel. The fastest way to success is to adopt the formula I outlined above.

Here is an idea. Before crossing my formula off as another piece of marketing mumbo-jumbo, give it a shot. Adapt this formula to fit your own personality and see for yourself if it is a waste of time.

38. Nobody Owes You a Living

The last 12 months may not have won any awards, but we are watching the months come and go like never before. I heard from a local country "hay seed" yesterday that this year's colorful scenery was due to a lack of water. Sounded plausible to me. Color today. Bare branches tomorrow. "And the seasons they go round and round." Reference to a Joni Mitchell tune. (Circle Game)

Regardless of the month or the Zodiac sign we still have time to look for ways to build our businesses and continue to move forward with some semblance of positivity. And we can use every minute we have.

We have time to find and help more people begin planning their dreams while we introduce ourselves to more upbeat, fun, proactive folks out there in marketing land.

For many of you this is alarming news since you have been leaning on and blaming both summer and Covid-19 for the reason your business has taken a hit. Some agents felt it best to back-off during the midst of the Covid-19 Pandemic as a way to give their prospects some breathing room. I agree... kind of.

I have come to learn that nobody owes me a living. And likewise, nobody owes you a living. What you do about your business is your business. But please, do not think for a moment that your competition is going to take the rest of the year off. Because some of them won't.

Please do not misinterpret my suggestion. I am not inferring that you become an arrogant, manipulative, sleazy, fast-talking, replication of yesterday's sales bag, or should I say "sleaze bag." Quite the contrary. I want you to leap out of bed tomorrow morning with the intention of brightening up somebody's day. I once reminded you that a few choice words directed at the right person can indeed make a positive and uplifting impression. Never underestimate the power of your kind words.

What are you waiting for? Starting tomorrow morning get up and direct a few choice words toward your customers, prospects, ex-clients and preferred suppliers. Do what you can to bring a little sunshine to their world.

The operative word starting tomorrow is "**ACTION**." It really doesn't matter what you do as long as you do "something."

39. Don't Bite Off More Than You Can Chew

The following advice may sound elementary, mundane, or even amateurish to some of you. It isn't. Trying to do too much too soon is an exercise in futility. **Bottom Line:** Don't bite off more than you can chew.

I tell you this because in a few short months, you will once again be writing down the things you are not going to accomplish in the year ahead. Hence, my advice to you today is very timely.

With reference to your next to-do list, I have a better idea. I have a more realistic idea. I have a more logical idea. Why not write an "I plan to list" that has a genuine chance to work in your favor? Write down just **two** goals to work on.

For example:
1. Slowly build your current "good-guy" customer list by adding 12 more "good guys." For the sake of argument, "good guy" translates to "profitable." Just 12. One every four weeks. If you find yourself adding more names, don't panic. Just accept your good fortune.

2. Budget for some personal development. If you need a number, how does $250 sound? Now, you won't have to

hesitate to buy a book, attend a course, join a webinar or subscribe to a personal development magazine. You can make Barnes & Noble your favorite coffee shop while they still exist. Since you have already budgeted for such luxurious expenses, it won't hurt at all. And there is no roll-over. If you don't spend this budget, you will lose it.

I know I said two, but here is a bonus item:
For the next two and a half months, work hard, honest and smart. The rest will fall into place, and you will find the days, weeks and months ahead will be kind to both you and your bank account.

I'm on a roll. Number four suggests that you "dump" five clients who are driving you nuts. The easiest way to do this without undue stress is to simply raise your management fee. Chances are they will eliminate themselves.

I'm going to skip a potential number five. But if I was forced to add a fifth, it would involve listing the ways you can have more fun. Starting today, start with #5.

40. Choose Your Words Wisely

This particular topic popped into my head early this morning for no apparent reason. I awoke to find myself thinking about words, phrases and sentences that were directed my way over the years.

You never know how your words may be taken by the recipient. For example, I don't think I will ever forget a particular sentence tossed my way by my college football coach back in 1968. I will spare you the specifics, but let it suffice to say, I have laid awake many nights reliving that particular brow beating.

Fast forwarding to the present I will try to shed some light on word choice by sharing a few more examples:

1. Saying "thank you" instead of simply saying "thanks" may appear as a little thing but in my mind conveys a vast difference in sincerity.
2. "Love ya" is a term used by many family members when terminating a phone call. "I love you" removes any doubt and delivers this heartfelt message clearly.
3. When responding to a "thank-you" from others, the term "No problem" in my mind is weak and lacking sincerity. A

much better choice of words might sound like "You're welcome" or, "I am glad I could help."

You might think I am getting picky. I beg to differ. Your choice of words in any one particular instance can result in either moving closer or further away from developing a meaningful relationship with both prospects and current customers.

More often than not, a few more choice words will position you as the "real deal" and isn't that what you are looking to achieve?

On a different note, but in a similar vein, it is important to remember that not everyone has, or appreciates your sense of humor. I have been known to cross this line on more than one occasion only to be reminded by my wife.

I am not suggesting you put a tarp on your humor gene, but I am suggesting that you think twice before sharing that humorous one-liner that is aching to be released.

41. Execution

E-X-E-C-U-T-I-O-N is a nine-letter word that has much to do with why most companies (and individuals) fail to meet their full potential. Said more accurately, it is the lack of execution.

According to Webster's New World College Dictionary – execute– is defined as: [to carry out; perform; do.]

The issue is not a lack of knowledge. It is a shortage of **"do."** Try this for the next seven days: Focus on the – **DO** – ...... the concept of execution.

Author Tom Peters (*In Search of Excellence*) once said: "It is amazing to me how many people in the oil business fail to get the message that in order to strike oil you have to dig a hole."

Popular clichés remind us that "talk is cheap" and "after all is said and done ... more is said than done."

If you want to strike oil dig a hole. If you want to grow your business, introduce your services to more people.

I'm not suggesting that planning, thinking, reflecting, and strategizing are not necessary steps in establishing excellence. I am reminding you that sooner or later you will need to put your money where your mouth is and put your knowledge, skills and personality into motion and *execute your plan*.

Here is a four-pronged strategy you can start immediately:

1. Finish what you start.
2. Concentrate on "barking up the right tree."
3. Perform job-related tasks with confidence.
4. Do what you say you will do.

42. Marketing Strategy #7: The Interview

Tonight, I decided to feature one of my sixteen marketing strategies I share in my advanced training classes. I was prompted to do so after reading a SpeakerNetNews tip from Rebecca Morgan. The tip was titled... *The Interview*.

Do you remember Larry King? He was a slightly overweight man who sat on one side of a desk sporting a pair of fashionable suspenders and outdated eyeglasses. He would invite popular guests to his show to interview them. He asked questions without providing his opinion. His guests were the reason for tuning in.

Larry King was a well-recognized and respected TV personality and all he ever did was ask questions. In similar fashion, I could cite David Letterman, Johnny Carson, Jay Leno and today's Stephen Colbert ... all familiar names to some extent who prompt their guests to "share" experiences. Everybody who has trouble sleeping knows who they are.

In my programs I remind travel professionals they too can assume the role of interviewer. They too can become better known in their marketplace by simply inviting people to share their experiences and opinions with them. **The result:** You will become more visible while you build a reputation as someone who thoroughly knows the travel business.

Here is how this could work:

Step 1: You identify a reason for your interviews.
Your market is facing a challenge today. It is affecting your business like never before. It is called Covid-19. And you are interested in learning how it has altered your client's travel plans.

Step 2: Come up with a series of questions.
1. Have you had to cancel a trip in the last eight months? For what reason?
2. Are you planning to reschedule your trip?
3. Are you still hesitant to leave the safety of your home?
4. Do you feel the airlines have adequately safe-guarded future flights?
5. When will you feel it is safe to travel freely again?
6. Do you feel masks will become the norm when traveling?
7. Is your "bucket list" a thing of the past, or is there some destination you still dream about?

Step 3: You make a list of people to call.
Start with just three or four names so the task does not overwhelm you. You will soon add to this list as you find yourself actually enjoying these conversations ... while learning a great deal in the process.

Step 4: Make the call.

Call each person on your list and tell them you are writing an article involving current Travel Trends. You would love to hear their opinion on the subject. You then ask if you can "schedule" a better time to chat. Chances are they will be available to speak with you at that time, so be prepared with your list of questions.

Step 5: Take notes
This step is self-explanatory but make it clear how much you appreciate their input. Remember, you are not making a sales call. You are conducting a professional interview soliciting their candid thoughts on the subject.

If you maintain a friendly yet professional tone, chances are you will make a positive impression without appearing as hungry or pushy and out for personal gain. Don't be surprised when the person you are speaking with begins to ask you how you run your business, and if you might be in position to assist them with their future travel plans.

I realize your mind is probably spinning with the names of many people who would be prime candidates for your interviews.

43. Lessons From a Fabric Store

You are probably wondering if Marchev has gone off the deep end? No I haven't. Not yet. I want to share an observation I once had in a fabric store of all places.

My wife Barbara and I were strolling through a fabric store looking for decorating ideas when the subject of tonight's story hit me.

After being in the store for just a few minutes I felt a mild migraine coming on, and I don't get migraines! I was being introduced to the Three C's. Choices, colors and the associated *cost*. I must admit there was a lot of good-looking "stuff" in that store. In fact, my eyes started to glaze over as the myriad of styles, fabrics and colors began to overwhelm me. Apparently, choices, options, and colors are all needed to sell tile, carpets and related gizmos. (I really don't get migraines, but you can picture my oncoming chagrin.)

Here was what caught my attention and stopped me in my tracks. On top of one of the counters was a one-foot square tile sample. It was a mosaic pattern if I had to give it a name. My wife was drawn straight to this "sample." The store manager mentioned that two people purchased this exact mosaic pattern the day before as a result of spotting it on the counter. They saw it – they liked it - they bought it. (My wife spotted it, but she wasn't ready to buy yet).

My advice to the store manager was to display what she wanted to sell. Car dealers have known this for years. Show room display cars sell *quickly*.

Vision is a strong selling feature. People buy what they can "see."

It helps if you can paint a picture. Any picture. A fun picture. Tell the story, *your* story, in *your* words, but in words that can paint a picture in the buyer's mind. Let people "see" what you are talking about. This particularly holds true with exciting and exotic travel destinations.

Toss in a little sincere enthusiasm and some good things are about to come your way.

Take it from me. Pictures sell.

44. Are You Climbing Up the Wrong Ladder?

If you have been reading any of my daily articles over the last four years, you know I have a penchant for the "analogy." *(Comparison; similarity; equivalence between independent parts; a form of reasoning.)*

A recent idea came to me while I was climbing to my roof to replace a few loose shingles torn by a passing windstorm.

You probably never stopped to focus on it, but ladders are potentially dangerous constructs. Notice how many "warning" labels are glued to the sides of your ladder. Just like Jim Croce recommended in song "not to mess around with Jim," I'm telling you not to mess around with ladders.

But ladders are both useful and in demand once you determine that your goal, or objective is slightly out of reach. You select a tool to help achieve your purpose. Enter: the ladder.

You lean the ladder up against a supporting wall and begin to climb. Step-by-step you position your foot on each rung, while always maintaining balance until you elevate yourself into a targeted position.

NOTE: I failed to mention that prior to ascending, (1) you take the time to check and double check ensuring the base of your ladder is firmly positioned and rock steady, and then (2) you have somebody help steady your ladder as you begin to climb.

"Mike, enough already. Shingles. Roof. Ladder. What's the message in this article?"

Now that you've got my ladder scenario firmly embedded in your head. I want you to picture the ladder as a means to an end. Most of you already have your ladder in place, and most of you are moving up in the right direction. But many of you might have your ladder positioned on the "wrong wall." You will soon get to the top, but it just might be the wrong top.

You may be climbing your own ladders hoping to achieve success. (In this case your ladder represents your marketing plans.) But there is also a good chance that you have placed your ladder against the wrong wall. You are busy striving to achieve the wrong objective.

Let's net this out. (1) Select the **RIGHT** destination. Make sure you are pursuing your intended objective; (2) Choose the **RIGHT** tools, (ladder/marketing gambits) (3) Take each step one at a time while always maintaining your balance. (4) Be aware that any misstep could result in some serous discomfort. (5) Don't begin to climb until you are convinced you are on firm ground. (6) Don't multi-task while climbing your ladder.

FOCUS. CONCENTRATE. PAY ATTENTION.

45. Repetition Is Not a Bad Thing

Tonight's message came to me the other day while I was trying to come up with a clever title for a new article.

I couldn't help but reflect on a recent article I wrote using the crossword puzzle as an analogy. It was "spot on." I wanted to share it again, but perhaps with a slightly different twist. Rather than sound like a broken record, I decided to come up with something "new."

That is when I took a break to sit down at the piano and played three songs I have been working on. I noticed I was playing each more fluidly while thinking less about my next chord change. My playing was sounding a lot more like music. How did that happen?

I realized that my musical improvement had everything to do with *repetition*.

If I haven't lost you by now, here is tonight's message: Practice. Never stop practicing. When you think you have something down pat, practice some more. I am reminded of a quote from an NFL Hall of Famer who played for the Los Angeles Rams, Merlin Olsen. The big guy once said, **"If I am** not practicing and my competitor is, when we meet, they will beat me."

I have been quoted as saying the difference between in amateur and a professional is amateurs do things when they want to. A professional does things when it is time to.

A professional never stops practicing. He or she recognizes the value of doing the right thing at the right time in the right order over and over again. And to pull this off consistently one must practice beyond boredom or fatigue. The term "muscle memory" comes to mind.

I have often been reminded while teaching graduate school students that I have adopted a nonlinear delivery style. I hope that you can follow my often-times bouncing train of thought.

One last point. Practice alone does not make perfect. Practice makes permanent. Practicing the right things makes perfect.

46. Are You Protecting Your Greatest Asset?

The latest audible book I am listening to is by Greg McKeown titled **Essentialism**. It is about understanding what is essential while discounting the rest. I listen to a chapter every night while lying in bed ready to call it a day.

When I heard the phrase, "Are you protecting your assets?" I sat up and made a note to myself immediately.

It has been said by many people that **YOU** are the product in a service organization. **YOU** are the true differentiating factor. **YOU** are the reason in a me-too industry people select you as their service advisor.

Advice from Navy Seals training reminds candidates, **"A dead man cannot save anybody."** This is a succinct way of reminding us that we must ensure that we are in a solid position and in good health if we are going to help anybody. **YOU** first.

Flight attendants remind us to secure our own oxygen masks before going to the aid of our children. This may sound selfish, but it is the prudent thing to do. The reasoning is exactly the same. **YOU** first, so you can help second.

If **YOU** are the differentiating feature of your company, that makes **YOU** a true asset. That means **YOU** must be worthy of protection.

It is high time that you start paying more attention to **you**, your strengths, your capabilities, your frame of mind and your never-ending opportunities to be of service to your targeted audience. Did I mention your health, your emotional intelligence and your sense of humor?

If you are not actively helping your clients, then it is time you continue to help yourself. This can be accomplished by (1) reading, writing, attending workshops, (2) watching supplier webinars while taking time to internalize your notes, (3) meeting with prospects and asking questions, (4) brainstorming with your peers, and (5) joining like-minded business-development groups. Little-by-little. Step-by-step. **You** first.

YOU are an asset. Make no mistake about it. **You** are worth protecting. Make no mistake about it. Recognize that you are a true asset to your clients. Make no mistake about that. Decide what needs doing to become a better **YOU**. Then begin improving and adding to your value each and every day.

47. Don't "Throw In The Towel?" Not Yet!

Having always considered myself a realist, I have a few thoughts to share about "throwing in the towel." And make no mistake about it. The day is coming when those exact four words may very well appear as an attractive option. And yes. I have been known to utter these four words myself. (Shame on me.)

I fear the day when you are going to feel the full brunt of all your "useless" efforts. That's the day you will want to call it quits, and "throw in the towel." This will not be the action of a sore loser, but as a conscious decision from a hard-working, good intentioned entrepreneur who feels their efforts have all been for naught for the past twelve months.

The term "emotional intelligence" just flashed across my mind, but that is not what I want to talk about today. I also will avoid repeating what you have been hearing from a hundred other "know-it-alls" when all this doubt first entered your mind. In the interest of time, and in an attempt to protect my reputation for "shooting-from-the-hip," I will say what I came to say.

When the going gets tough, (and it really doesn't get any tougher than it is right now) there is not a man, woman or child alive today who will not entertain the decision to give up, cry uncle, turn the page, roll the dice in a new direction and quite simply, "throw in the towel." I would be less than honest if I said I have not tussled with this decision myself on a number of occasions the past few months. I often feel I am "spinning my wheels." I guess there is something to the statement, "We are all in this together."

For a few of you, if the truth be known, "throwing in the towel" would prove to be a wise decision. Many "travel advisors" joined our industry for the love of travel. They are not, have not, and will never pay the price for true service professionalism. The game board has been altered significantly, and I am afraid only the cream will rise to the top.... as it has been known to do.

But most of you provide a valuable service and will continue to do so when the pendulum starts swinging back through some semblance of "normal." I wish I could tell you when that will be. I can't.

I have no idea of your financial position, or your relationship with your clients and loved ones. What I do know is this:
1. Your homerun may be coming with the very next pitch. (A single, double or triple would also be welcome.)
2. What you are dealing with at the moment is not strictly confined to you.
3. You did not get this far in life by accident.
4. Brighter days lie ahead.
5. I think I know that throwing in the towel, although an alluring option at times, and perhaps one appearing more and more attractive, may not be the right move at this time.

I can't help believing that your clients are "chaffing at the bit" when it comes to cabin fever and the urge to get out of town again. Your career will soon begin to blossom. But in order to "blossom" you must be ready, willing and able to spring into action once the light turns green. Your job to educate your clients and help them make better travel-related decisions will once again be in demand… and very much valued. My advice: Hold on to that towel for just a little longer.

48. Three "Brilliant" Reminders

Get ready for a curve ball. Here it comes.

In over four years of writing a daily column for Travel Research Online, I have never done what I am about to do. (Don't you just love the suspense.) I am about to introduce you to something new.

No, I am not going to write this article while riding an elephant naked down Atlantic Avenue in Delray Beach, Florida. (I'm just wondering after reading that last sentence, if you envisioning a naked elephant, or an old guy with no clothes on? Just asking!

Instead, I am going to share three of my favorite quotes with you. Each one consists of a few words of wisdom that have me pausing and reflecting before moving on.

#1: "If I am not practicing and my competitor is, when we meet, they will beat me."

Merlin Olsen, Former NFL Football Hall of Famer hit the nail right on the head with this one. Practice, repetition, trial and error is the name of the game if you want to gain entry into your personal hall-of-fame. The good news is that most people do not, and will not, have the discipline to continue practicing once they feel it is time to stop practicing. You can follow the leaders in any endeavor, and you will see the same thing. The winners will be recognized for their discipline when it comes to practice.

#2: It is amazing to me how many people in the oil business fail to get the message, in order to strike oil you have to dig a hole."

Tom Peters, co-author of In Search of Excellence shared this poignant reminder. Most people talk about it, plan about it, think about it, dream about it, brainstorm about it, and do everything, they can to avoid doing something about it. If you want to find oil, dig a hole. If by chance you hit an empty hole, dig another one.

I am not suggesting you approach any worthwhile program with wild abandonment or a lack of respect. I do endorse a certain degree of planning and thinking about your next move.

But to avoid insulting your intelligence, I will leave this message up to you. I will give you a hint. **Less talk – more action.**

One more ... #3. Howard Cosell once interviewed Jimmy "The Greek" Snyder. (A lawyer and a "bookie.")

When asked what he liked best in life, Jimmy quickly responded with, **"I like to win."** The follow up question was, "What do you like second best in life?" Just as quickly Jimmy responded with, **"That's easy Howard. I like to lose."**

What "The Greek" was saying in no uncertain terms that day was **he lived for the action**. He knew he would sometimes win a bet. He also knew he would experience his share of losing. But it was "the action" that kept his juices flowing, and his mind in the game.

Are you too concerned about winning ...at all times ...at all costs? Or, are you allowing "the action" to be your drug of choice?

I can hear some of you saying, "That all sounds very fine Marchev, but I would have preferred the naked elephant scenario."

I am hoping your dreams tonight do not include a naked man riding an elephant down Main Street. If so, please accept my apologies.

49. Some Good Advice for Job Seekers

If you have been reading my articles you probably find yourself disagreeing with me from time to time. If you find yourself disagreeing with me more often than not, I suggest you stop reading and go pursue the pastime of your choice. This is known as emotional intelligence.

But even if you do agree with my opinions now and then, I just may test your loyalty with tonight's story.

First of all, I am not a big fan of the job resume. That statement, in and of itself may sound sacrilegious to some of you. Remember, tonight's story is being written by a "maverick." I feel that the time spent crafting and editing a detailed document outlining your qualifications and how "really cool" you are is more or less a waste of time. I say this because your resume is literally one of hundreds that look and sound EXACTLY the same. In my opinion the resume is the ideal tool to make the selection process a whole lot easier for the decision maker by helping to disqualify candidates quickly and without much thought.

You must admit all resumes look alike and sound pathetically similar. The job seeker often forgets that although the reader may appear to be in a position of authority, they too feel they are over-worked and under-paid. Eliminating candidates is far easier than separating fact from fiction. Especially when the wrong selection could cost them their jobs.

If you are open to hearing a professional opinion that is reality-based and designed to capture the attention, as well as the imagination of the decision maker, I say, *lose the resume*.

In any sales situation, regardless of the service, product or industry, step one calls for capturing the buyer's attention. This won't happen if you insist on playing the same ole "pick me" resume game. You must step away from normal mob behavior and position yourself as "**someone special**" right from the get-go.

Here is what I suggest you do the next time you want to start work on Monday.

First, decide what gives your future supervisor (your boss) their biggest headache. Regardless of the industry or day of the week, I will now tell you exactly what that is.
(1) They want an employee they can count on; one that will come to work ready to work every day ... on time ... with a semblance of a personality.
(2) They want an employee who does not come with an attitude. They are looking for people who are "coachable" and who have a keen desire to improve.
(3) They are looking for an employee who is willing to contribute and will professionally represent both the company and their boss. A sense of humor never hurts either.

Everything else can be taught in very short order.

Here is what I want you to write to your next potential employer:

My name is Mike Marchev. After researching XYZ's latest accomplishments and plans for the future, I have come to the realization that 1) I believe I can personally contribute to the growth or your organization, and 2) If given the opportunity to do so, you will not regret your decision. How can I say this?
(1) I will show up ready to work every day .... on time. (Everyday)
(2) I am a team player. I am coachable and receptive to input.
(3) I will perform my duties without exception and without excuse. How soon can I begin proving my worth to you?

And Then There Is Sales

To those who are not looking for a new job, this same strategy holds true when trying to sell a new client on your services. Refrain from waxing eloquent. Tell the prospect the four things you can provide as soon as your business-relationship begins.

Simple sells. Truth sells. Results sell.

50. Cool Your Jets!

This next quote was taken from the book **To Sell Is Human** by Daniel Pink.

"It is an excess of assertiveness and zeal that leads to contacting customers too frequently. Extroverts often stumble over themselves. They talk too much and listen too little... which can be read as pushy and drive people away."

For years it was believed that successful sales personnel exhibited an outgoing, people-oriented, fun, and vivacious personality. Sales pros had one thing in common, and that was the "gift-of-gab." They could mix and mingle with anybody at a moment's notice. (Keep this to yourself, but forty years ago I failed a test for a high-level sales job because I was not considered extroverted enough. Bummer!)

As consumers were given access to more information and became smarter as a result of their own research, less demand was placed on the extrovert of yesterday when it came to selling. In fact, today's successful sales professional might even border on the introverted side of life. They talk less and listen more. (It appears I was perhaps, ahead of my time.)

The pushy, aggressive, master of the "close" salesperson has fast become yesterday's news. Slowing down. Backing off.

Asking more meaningful questions and taking the time to listen while internalizing the feedback is the key to more sales.

Here is my message today: Slow down. Stop talking. Start listening. Begin selling.

51. In Search of That Elusive "One Thing"

One of my favorite movie clips came from the movie City Slickers. Billy Crystal was riding alongside the tough-guy cattle herder played by Jack Palance. (Curly)

Curly said the secret to life was just **One Thing** as he held up his pointer finger. Crystal was all ears as that was exactly what he wanted to learn from the crusty old cowboy. "What's the one thing?" he asked. "That is what you have to find out," answered Curly, as he rode out of frame.

For many, the hope of finding the "one thing" will come in the form of a magic pill. There seems to be a pill for just about everything these days ... from headaches to pain to weight loss to cholesterol control ... to unforeseen "intimate moments" for you old guys. Yet most sales and marketing gurus, coaches and trainers are quick to remind you that there is no "magic pill" when it comes to business success.

There is not "one thing" that works for everybody. But you do have something at your beck-and-call that will work for you. It is not generic. It is your personal brand. And therein lies the rub. Just like Curly shared with Billy the city boy, you have to discover it for yourself. You have to find it. You have to polish it. You have to use it. You have to learn from it. You have to work at it.

Your "one thing" is different from mine. Mine is different from yours.

The "one thing" comes in different sizes, colors, shapes and styles. The single common denominator is that all "one things" usually fall under the umbrella known as **m-a-r-k-e-t-i-n-g**. They all involve getting the right people to know you, like you, and eventually trust you. Whichever "strategy" you choose to use, you must do so daily ... without exception ... without excuses ... or your "one thing" will soon become just "another thing."

"**One Things**" take the form of networking; emailing; written communications; public speaking; blogs; websites; contests; demonstrations; home parties; proposals; collaborations etc. Your "one thing" is no better than mine. It just is a better fit for your budget, time constraints and personality. And your "one thing" is the "one thing" that works for you. As long as you practice your "one thing" daily you have a good chance at enjoying the results.

As you prepare to call it another day, I challenge you to find, begin developing and refining your own **"One Thing."**

I also challenge you to do something that you may have been avoiding for the past ten months. Try with every fiber of your body to have more "*FUN*" in the months ahead. Now that sounds like the "one thing" I can buy into.

52. From Annoying Pest to Welcome Guest

I recently received three emails from members of my Inner Circle Group asking me to critique their recent attempts of drafting sales letters.

In all three cases I spotted a common mistake as well as a few other errors which I felt compelled to comment on. Let's see if we all can learn something from my recent experience.

Because your topic probably is a subject you feel comfortable with there will be a tendency to write about your qualifications, sincerity and interest at the expense of the more important focal point. **THE READER.**

Here are a few of my suggestions. (If the shoe fits, wear it.) If I am not talking to you, stop reading and get back to brushing your teeth.

1. Decide whom you want to write to.
2. Determine what you think they **want** to hear.
3. Decide what you want them to do as a result of reading your letter.

Once you have a feel for the above three steps, begin jotting down possible answers. This simple exercise will help you focus on what is important. This task will soon take shape and become easier as you continue to *draft* your thoughts.

After completing your first draft, I want you to perform the following exercise. Count the number of times you refer to yourself vs them. I, my, we, us vs. you, yours, them, theirs.

Remember …
1. Nothing positive can happen if your letter does not get read.
2. They will not read your letter if they don't feel there is something in it for them.
3. They don't give a hoot about you.

Assume, (and correctly so) your readers will be asking themselves these questions: A. What's in it for me? B. Why should I care? C. What's the upside of doing what you are asking me to do?

I don't believe there is an answer to the question: "How does one write a sales letter that works?" There are too many variables at any given point in time to hang your hat on just one hook. I am afraid I have to say what you do not want to hear. "**Trial and error.**"

Test your letters and see for yourself what works. Just hedge your bets by NOT shooting yourself in the foot by making common mistakes of self-interest.

I'll end message #52 by sharing the salesman's mantra which encompasses both letter writing and in-person presentations: **BE BRIGHT; BE BRIEF; BE GONE.**

53. Follow Up Never Goes Out of Style

When I started thinking about retirement, Barbara and I began investigating log cabin homes. We did what any investigators might do ... purchase a log home magazine at the supermarket and send away for all the free stuff that was not nailed down. Send we did. Stuff we got.

But here is where tonight's lesson begins.

I am absolutely appalled at the lack of professionalism shown by the log home industry. Sure, they got an "A" for sending stuff just the way every other company gets an "A" for sending stuff from direct mail, trade shows, etc. This is the easy part.

But as the weeks passed and I had not received one phone call following up my clear sign of "interest," I began to think less of the industry.

Haven't log cabin salespeople ever been introduced to the Rule of 7? Didn't anybody tell them the importance of appearing a little interested in potential buyers? Don't they realize that I just might have a few other things to think about during the course of any given day and that I might appreciate a little attention from an expert home specialist?

I had no idea that log cabins were such in demand that all you need to do is shoot out a few catalogs and take orders.

The smart log cabin salespeople (by my definition) would spot a guy who raised his hand silently indicating:

"I'll bite. Teach me something."

They would then follow the catalog with an easy-to-read brochure or email explaining how a septic system works in the middle of the woods or how to dig a hole in your backyard and find water, or how to squeeze a little "juice" from an electric pole to a remote location ... or how to shoo bears off your back porch, or how to bake biscuits on a wood-burning stove and/or 1001 other trinkets of information that a rube from New Jersey might find useful prior to sticking himself, along with his family on top of a hill in upstate New York. (Enough about me and my housing conundrum. What about you?)

When you witness a potential client raising their hand, do you seize the opportunity by plugging them into a logical follow-up program? I certainly hope so. Because if you don't, these very same would-be clients might be bad-mouthing you as an uneducated professional who isn't motivated enough to play the game the way it is designed to be played. This is not the ideal situation.

I am not talking about becoming overly aggressive, pushy, arrogant or sleazy. I am inferring that you show a little interest and professionalism.

Remember:

When you are out of sight, you are out of mind. ***The Rule of 7 indicates that you must follow up more than once.

It is not their job to follow up. It is yours. The Rule of 7 reminds us that in order to do business with somebody who is not familiar with you takes a number of contacts over time to gain traction in the relationship. The key point is that consistency and persistence will pay dividends moving forward.

54. What Do Gutters Have to Do with Anything?

Have you noticed there are more commercials on television these days promoting the benefits of protecting your home from gutter leaks?

What I find interesting about these advertisements is their focal point. It became clear to me almost immediately that they were not referencing how dried leaves backup in gutters and can clog the downspout. Water then builds up and backs up until it freezes.

Then the fun begins. Ice creeps up the roof and soon, with the sun and the warmth coming from inside your home, the ice melts and finds its way into the under layers of your roof, and down into your ceiling. The damage resulting to your internal ceilings and walls can easily add up to thousands of dollars. Not much good results from clogged gutters.

These ads do not mention the damage ice can cause as a result of a backed-up gutter. There are not many products on the market today less sexy than gutter shields. A toilet plunger comes to mind, but let's not go there.

The ads shed light on the dangers involved in climbing a ladder. They focus on the safety aspect of one's annual ascent to your roof's water trough. In addition to falling off an unstable ladder, it is not uncommon to cut your hand while scraping through the aluminum channel for soggy, decaying dead leaves, sharp twigs and all sorts of nasty debris.

What does this observation have to do with you? I see a lesson here hiding behind your gutter shield. Are you, or do you spend most of your limited "airtime" talking about the destination and means of getting there and back? Or, do you see the value in focusing on your prospect's underlying true interests?

Clearing a gutter or two once a year is no big deal. But schlepping a rickety ladder out of your garage, around to the back of your house, finding a pair of old work gloves, making sure the ladder is stable, picking a day that is not too cold or windy, and bagging the rotten, moldy, wormy decaying leaves so they can be picked up by your town's garbage collector on Wednesday sounds like work to me.

I hope you made the connection to ALL the work that goes into booking a vacation these days considering all the unknown variables and health/safety considerations.

You are not selling a destination. You are selling peace-of-mind. You are selling attention to detail. You are selling peace of mind knowing that everything which needs attention has been attended to. You are selling the notion that you are removing all forms of ladders and unknowns from the equation and paving the way for nothing but smooth sailing.

I don't want a gutter shield. I want to know I don't have to climb up on the roof again.

55. My Thoughts on Integrity Selling

"PEOPLE ARE MORE APT TO BELIEVE YOU WHEN THEY SEE A CONGRUENCE BETWEEN WHAT YOU SAY AND WHO YOU ARE."

(A quote taken from the book Integrity Selling: How to Succeed in Selling in the Competitive Years Ahead — by Ron Willingham, page 99.)

For years sales professionals had a reputation of saying what their prospects wanted to hear, and then resorting back to business as usual. Politicians have honed this skill to perfection.

The sad truth is that this poor reputation has been earned over the years. That is why most people, regardless of the industry, do not cozy up to the notion of "selling." Salespeople cannot be trusted. Salespeople have their own agenda. Salespeople talk too much and listen far too little. Salespeople disappear as soon as the sale is made.

You are a salesperson. How does this make you feel? I am a salesperson and I know how it makes me feel. Insulted.

Buyers are not stupid. They are very familiar with salespeople and how the poor ones operate by chasing their quotas and trying every trick in the book to:
1) Overcome objections
2) Upsell their products, and
3) Close every deal they can for the most profit.

But you are not like this. You are a good, honest, hardworking, caring person whose single goal is to help people make better buying decisions when it comes to travel. The fastest and most reliable way to position yourself as the good person you are is to "walk your talk." Be real. Show your prospects and clients a congruence between what you say and who you are.

To borrow from another book I once wrote, **BECOME THE EXCEPTION**

56. "Lazy" Is Not a Flattering Characteristic

I was speaking with a seasoned travel professional the other day when he mentioned something that caught my attention. He shared a recent event with me. He was having lunch with a group of agency owners who shared the same affiliation when a common thread emerged from the conversation.

He said all but one in the group mentioned that over the last ten months they have become lazy when it came to focusing on their businesses. They were having trouble getting back on track and performing the daily tasks that twelve months ago came naturally. They had lost or were losing their passion as each day unfolded.

For obvious reasons they now had time to concentrate on more personal activities and found enjoyment in performing non-work activities. This came as no surprise to me as the last twelve months have affected us all in deeply personal ways.

He went on to mention a concept that I am all too familiar with. He said that he felt it was high time to get back to basics. One word shot into my mind at this point.
BRILLIANT!

The first step in achieving difficult tasks is to recognize the fact that perhaps you have been selling yourself short. Call it being lazy or call it lacking motivation. As you ponder the conundrum, you just might refer to it as a lapse in direction or a failure to see the big picture.

All that we have been experiencing over the past months and all we have been doing other than providing travel-related services paints a clear backdrop for the problem at hand.

Today I will simply say that becoming lazy is not something you invented. We all have been lazy to some degree. It has become another by-product of COVID-19. By simply recognizing this less-than-attractive behavior you (we) are well on our way to filing it as soon-to-be **"yesterday's news."**

Becoming lazy in times like these may be considered a common practice but it should in no way, shape or form be construed as a good thing. A sure-fire way to begin shaking yourself out of what appears to be lazy behavior is to begin accumulating "small" wins again. Start recognizing and enjoying the little things you are doing right.

In tomorrow night's story I will share a few of my own ideas on how to overcome the laziness factor.

57. Are You Becoming Lazy? Part Two

I recently shared what I believed to be a common conundrum among travel professionals as COVID-19 continued to hinder people's travel plans. To be more specific, there seems to be a tendency for us all to become "tired" when it comes to performing the needed duties associated with building a business.

At the root of the problem is the fact that for the past twelve months we have found the time to enjoy the tasks that we consider to be more fun, more rewarding, and less frustrating or stressful.

Although we have succumbed to the problem, we now must "snap out of it" to borrow a phrase from the movie **MOONSTRUCK** staring Cher and Nicholas Cage.

In simple terms, becoming less lazy calls for being more active. So, the question surfaces: How can we do what needs doing and actually enjoy the process? The answer is simple: By doing what works and what pays visible dividends.

The initial step is to begin envisioning your business as what it truly can be. You can rebound and become a profitable entity, if that is what you really want to happen. Then it becomes a matter of "small wins." Logically follow the path that will lead you to profitability. And this brings me to my ear-torn, surefire piece of advice that you can take to the bank. **"Become more visible."** Like it or not, you must come out of hiding and put yourself on the firing line. You must be seen. You must bring your assets to your marketplace. You must be heard. You must openly and freely share your knowledge with those who are interested.

I sometimes find that a simple change of pace and/or direction is enough to put a little bounce back in my step. A phone call to an upbeat friend or associate often is enough to reignite my "mojo." Perhaps a podcast is in your future. The options are all available .... and up to you.

But once you begin "experimenting" again and hitting on a few success stories, your energies will kick back into high gear and before you know it you will be doing your "happy dance" once again. (Remember, you must dance like nobody's watching.)

Lazy is for slugs, and you are not a slug. All you might require is a little nudging in the right direction to get you back in the game. Little wins. Step-by-step. Always moving toward your target. Tomorrow will soon be one of the "good ole days."

The good ole days are still in front of us.

Five of My Favorite Quotes:

"If my pitcher would pitch in the beginning of the game the same way he pitches at the end of the game once he realizes he is losing, he would not be losing in the first place." Casey Stengel, NY Mets Baseball Manager

"It is amazing to me how many people in the oil business fail to get the message that in order to strike oil you have to dig a hole." Tom Peters, Author of In Search of Excellence

"If I am not practicing and my competitor is, when we meet, he/she will beat me." Merlin Olsen, NFL All-Pro Lineman

"Of the nearly eight billion people residing on our planet I can split them into just two groups. (A) Those people I can help ... and (B) The other kind." Mike Marchev, Author of Become The Exception

When Italian Olympic downhill heartthrob and presumed gold medalist was asked what went wrong on his last run down the mountain, he simply replied, *"I fell"* before slowly skiing off. (No excuses.)

www.ingramcontent.com/pod-product-compliance
Lightning Source LLC
Chambersburg PA
CBHW071832210526
45479CB00001B/98